CANDY MEN

The Story of Switzer's Licorice

Patrick Murphy

Library of Congress Control Number: 2020938239

ISBN: 9781681062761

Cover design: Eric Marquard
Page design: Claire Ford

Printed in the United States of America
20 21 22 23 24   5 4 3 2 1

DEDICATION

To Annie, my Sweetie.

Switzer's
Yellow Jacket
MOLASSES CANDY.

Chew Mint Leaf Gum.

TABLE OF CONTENTS

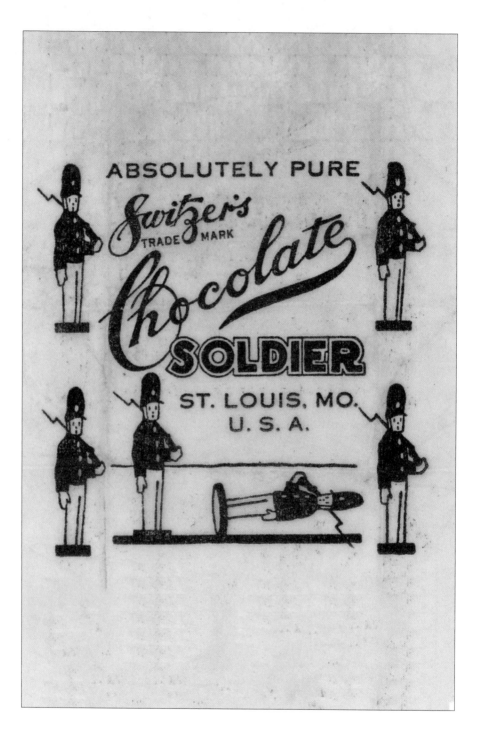

*Wrapper for the Chocolate Soldier, a popular bite-sized candy,
1920s. Photo courtesy of Switzer's Licorice Archive.*

ACKNOWLEDGMENTS

Having spent the past 30 years writing for television, I was surprised how ill-prepared I was to write an actual book with pages and a cover. A book, I have learned, is very different from a television show. I owe a great debt of gratitude to the following people for helping me navigate this strange, new land.

My wife, Anne Murphy, was the first to convince me that there was a real story among these ragged scraps of family history. With her keen eye for detail, she smoothed many of the rough spots, and her loving reassurance pulled me more than once from the brink of despair.

My good friend Dan Warner shares my love of history and licorice. From his extensive collection of historic images and anecdotes, Dan has created a Switzer's Licorice Archive, which he has graciously shared.

Writing this book gave me excuses to connect with my Switzer cousins and confirm that the Murphys didn't just make this stuff up. Michael Switzer, a true marketing talent, shared his story of resurrecting the family legacy. Tom Switzer, with his love of genealogy, brought the past back to life with long-forgotten stories and rare family photos. Fred Switzer III was generous in sharing his memories of family and business matters. My cousin Harriet Switzer is a remarkable woman. Over the course of her life, she has been a debutante, a religious of the Society of the Sacred Heart, teacher and Head of Villa Duchesne, President of Maryville University, and Secretary to the Board of Trustees of Washington University. Her insights into the character of her family made this a better book.

Jim Clark, with the sharp, analytical mind of a scientist, retold the story of his struggle to maintain quality taste and texture while incorporating new technologies into the manufacturing of licorice.

Bob Kill graciously looked back though a half century of his life in the food business to talk about his days as a young executive tasked with the responsibility of taking Switzer's Licorice from a family business into the big-time corporate world.

I also owe my gratitude to Joe Scalzitti for sharing his stories of those who fought to keep the brand alive in the competitive world of international candy deals.

The Missouri History Museum, the *St. Louis Post-Dispatch*, and the St. Louis Public Library are known for the patience and perseverance of their staffs in helping the wayward researcher. I am thankful to them for getting me what I needed, even when I wasn't certain what that might be.

Preservationist and historian Michael Allen and developer Pete Rothschild filled a number of gaps in the story of the old factory's last days.

I am particularly indebted to my new friends at Reedy Press. In television we tell stories by not letting the words get in the way of the pictures. Josh Stevens, Barbara Northcott, and the Reedy team patiently taught me that the opposite applies in publishing.

Finally, I owe special thanks to my great uncle Fred Murphy, who actually lived most of this story and did his best to preserve the best parts of it in the hope that someone, someday, might find it interesting.

PREFACE

There was a time when the blocks along the St. Louis Riverfront were thick with the smell of licorice. It was heavy and sweet, almost medicinal, and that's the scent my father carried with him throughout my childhood. He told me that his father shared that same scent, as did his grandfather, who fled Ireland with little more than the experience he had working in his family's candy shop.

The St. Louis part of our story picks up in 1881, when Joseph Murphy married Margaret Switzer and started a candy business with her younger brother Frederick. But I'm getting ahead of myself.

The following story is mostly true. It's the story of two Irish-American families whose faith in their future was founded on candy. Mostly true, because what really happened lies in a foggy place somewhere between the public records and a world of anecdotes and family myths. Both the Murphys and the Switzers have their memories, and they are surprisingly similar after so many years.

The story is cobbled together from interviews with members of the Switzer family and others, outside the family, who recall their dealings with the business. There are my own boyhood memories of visiting the factory and observing these "candy men," as they called themselves. A Murphy family treasure is an interview my father recorded with his Uncle Fred in 1967 in which Fred recalled growing up in St. Louis's Kerry Patch and working in the factory during the early years of the twentieth century. The clinking of ice cubes and freshening of glasses is still audible on the scratchy, old tapes.

The factory, with its giant Switzer's Licorice sign stretching along the wall beside the Eads Bridge, was a city landmark for decades. The building blew down in a storm in 2006, weakened by years of abandonment and neglect. But when it seemed the story was finally over, an unexpected twist created yet another chapter for Switzer's Licorice. So this is also a story of birth, death, and resurrection.

This book is for those who enjoy wandering through St. Louis history, and for those who like a good tale of the American Dream. If you are of a certain age that allows you the memory of that smell along the Riverfront or the taste of a black licorice bar or a cherry whip, I offer you this story about the families who created it.

CHAPTER ONE

Passages

Our story begins in Ireland.

Michael Switzer was born in the town of Rathkeale, County Limerick, in 1827. Seven hundred years of English rule had made Ireland one of the poorest places on earth. It was hard to imagine that conditions in that desperate country could get any worse, but in the 1840s the potato crops turned black and died. It was a time of mass hunger, and Limerick lost one-fifth of its population to starvation or emigration. Michael left for America in the summer of 1851.

Switzer clearly does not have the ring of a typical Irish surname. Michael's forbears, the Schweitzers, were originally from the Palatine in what is today Southern Germany. They traveled to England in 1709, intending to catch a boat to America. Many of their countrymen had already made the voyage and were sending back reports of cheap land and an absence of irritating aristocrats to tax them or draft them into the army. However, while still in England, the Schweitzers encountered a bureaucratic snafu and the authorities sidetracked them to Ireland. They eventually decided to put down roots there, and in 1745 they changed the spelling of their name to Switzer.

It took a century and a famine to finally get a Switzer from Ireland to America. Fresh off the boat from Limerick, Michael Switzer worked odd jobs while gradually drifting west. He ended up in Springfield, Illinois, where he met his future bride, Margaret Morkin, a young woman who had come from County Tipperary. They married in 1857.

Margaret had made the journey to America by herself while still in her teens. Before moving to Illinois, she lived in New York where, like so many young Irish women at the time, she worked as a servant. By 1854 she was established enough to send for her brother Patrick. She sent a letter to her mother that included twenty-five dollars for Patrick's passage to America, along with some no-nonsense travel advice.

She warned that Patrick should avoid strong drink on the stretch between Tipperary and England, and advised him, "In regard to man catchers in Liverpool, you must be cautious unless you meet some trusty neighbor from home, and that way never give your business to the hands of any person."

She also made specific recommendations. Patrick should bring a jug large enough for a daily allotment of three quarts of water and should pack a strong rope to tie his belongings to his berth or risk losing them in the constant tossing of the ship.

Because passage by ship from Liverpool to New York often took more than six weeks, she also recommended that he bring "about a stone and a half (20 pounds) of good butter with some good bacon and as much eggs as you can. Oaten bread baked with a small portion of flour will stand seaworthy. Also, some potatoes from Liverpool would be very necessary, some Herring also."

Passage to America was only somewhat safer than remaining in Ireland. The majority of emigrants could only afford to book steerage class. Shipwrecks, cholera, and typhus often claimed as many as one-fifth of those who attempted the voyage. Margaret knew that survival was not guaranteed on what the Irish called the "coffin ships."

"Dear Brother, keep your Courage," she wrote. "You must put a new face on you, what all men have to do coming to this New World. Have good faith. Never give up. Without faith it is impossible to please God and he that Believth (sic) Not Shall Be Condemned."

Margaret's warnings painted a vivid picture of the risks immigrants were willing to take for a chance at a new life. Her brother Patrick was among the lucky ones. He made it safely to

America. Records show that by 1865 he was living in New York, had married a woman by the name of Margaret Fogerty, also from County Tipperary, and had two children, Catherine and Michael.

Margaret Morkin Switzer, ca. 1880.
Photo courtesy of the Murphy Family.

Margaret Morkin and Michael Switzer, newly married in 1857, moved from Illinois to St. Louis and rented a flat on the edge of Kerry Patch, an Irish neighborhood several blocks northwest of downtown. The Patch, as it was called, was notorious for its gangs, crime, and poverty. Michael found work on the city's bustling levee. Although their life wasn't easy, it was better than what they had known in Ireland. In short time, they were confident enough in their future to start a family.

Then, unexpectedly, Michael died. The circumstances were reported in *The Daily Missouri Republican* on September 8, 1865:

> INQUESTS. Coroner O'Reily yesterday held two inquiries, the first of which was held on the body of a floater, found at the Keokuk packet landing, foot of Pine street. The name of the man was ascertained to be Michael Switzer, who contracted to unload the steamer R. Leonora on Tuesday last. While engaged in the work he became slightly intoxicated, and went back on the boat to take a sleep, and fell into the river. The jury returned a verdict of accidental drowning.

Margaret buried her husband at Holy Trinity Catholic Cemetery in North St. Louis, known at the time as the Poor Man's Catholic Cemetery.

Michael left his wife and four children in what the newspaper called "destitute circumstances." A fifth child, seven-year-old Johanna, had died just months earlier. Of the surviving children, Mary Ellen was the oldest at six-years. Three-year-old Catherine would not live to see her 10th birthday. Margaret Catherine was two years old. The youngest, Frederick Michael Switzer, was barely a month old.

The Switzers would face years of poverty in Kerry Patch. Margaret eventually found the means to open a small grocery store by the name of the Lime Shop. She taught her children that survival depended upon two things, hard work and loyalty to family. There was no way she could have known that in the years ahead, her family's story would be changed by the arrival of an Irish political refugee from Dublin.

And so our story returns to Ireland.

Several years before the Great Famine, a young tradesman from Belfast named Bernard Murphy moved south to Dublin. Bernard was Roman Catholic, and Dublin offered a friendlier climate to members of his faith. He married a woman named Catherine Everhart, and by 1840 they had opened a shop on Capel Street in downtown Dublin, selling cakes and candies.

The appearance of candy shops on European streets was a recent phenomenon. The opening of new trade routes had considerably reduced the price of sugar. New mechanical inventions such as the lozenge-maker made it possible for small manufacturers to produce candy at affordable prices. Prior to the early nineteenth century, people bought candy either for its purported medicinal value or, for those who had the means, as a luxury item. By the time Bernard and Catherine had opened their shop, confectioneries served everyone from working-class children

Looking east over St. Louis's manufacturing district, mid 1860s. Photo courtesy of the Library of Congress.

buying penny candies to ladies and gentlemen in search of sweet cakes and elaborate creations of chocolate cream.

Their shop was successful, but in 1845 the Famine began its seven-year ravage of Ireland. Before it was over, one million people would starve to death. Almost two million would emigrate — most of them to America. Dublin suffered less than the rest of the country due to an influx of landed gentry escaping the poverty of the countryside. They brought their fortunes with them, as well as their expectations that the city would provide them opportunities to spend their money on the finer things.

Within a few years, Bernard and Catherine opened two more shops just a short walk from the River Liffey. They had created a nineteenth century version of a chain store, going by the name of Murphy's Belfast Confectionery. Bernard wrote poems for his advertisements. The following, demonstrating the breadth of his literary talents, appeared in the April 8, 1845, edition of Dublin's *Freeman's Journal*:

> 'Tis custom now, at close of day,
> Before the hour of nine,
> To take a cup of Congou tea,
> With MURPHY'S MUFFINS fine.
> His Muffins are both pure and sweet,
> At morning, noon and even'
> And they are bought in CAPEL-STREET,
> At number ONE-FIVE-SEVEN.

He left no doubt regarding his attention to quality in an article he wrote for the same newspaper the following year. Titled "Most Important Notice to the Inhabitants of the South Side of the City," it assured readers, "Murphy is enabled to sell Lozenges, Comfits, and other Sweets of the newest, and most varied descriptions at a lower price than any house in Dublin - no matter where or how manufactured - under what name - French or otherwise!"

Catherine became the head of both the family and the business when Bernard died unexpectedly in 1849. Family lore has it that he suffered a heart attack while on a stroll across the O'Connell Street Bridge. It was a shocking blow to a family that had enjoyed a secure and comfortable life, even in the worst of times. Now more than ever, the family's survival would depend upon the success of their business under Catherine's direction. The youngest of four sons, Joseph Bernard Murphy, was born two years before Bernard died and would have no recollection of his father. His first memories were of working in his mother's shops, learning the craft of making tea cakes and candies in a country suffering mass starvation.

It was a tenuous middle-class life and, being the youngest of the brothers, he was last in line for whatever inheritance there might be. In his teens he became caught up in the cause of Irish nationalism. There was certainly no lack of grand failures in the history of that country to fire the imagination of a young man willing to trade the dreary life of a shopkeeper for the glory of dying for Ireland.

The Rebellion of 1798, inspired by the American Revolution, was a disaster that claimed 30,000 Irish lives. The failed Young Irelander Rebellion of 1848 was still a recent memory. And in the spring of 1867, the so-called Fenian Uprising brought revolt to much of the country, including the outskirts of Dublin.

Joseph Murphy was 20 years old when that uprising brought a skirmish to a village within walking distance of his home on Capel Street. The Fenians were a brotherhood of idealistic young Irishmen committed to independence from Great Britain. Many years later, Joseph's son Fred would recall stories his father told him of how he and a band of rebels, armed only with sticks and rocks, attacked British forces in a battle that sounded very much like the Fenian attack in the nearby village of Tallaght.

Irish rebel and candy man Joseph Bernard Murphy, late 1870s. Photo courtesy of the Murphy Family.

The plan was to stage an uprising just beyond the city limits that would entice the British troops to leave their barracks in Dublin to suppress the rebellion. Their absence would, according to the plan, embolden the Dublin citizenry to stage its own insurrection. On March 5, 1867, more than 8,000 young men marched from Dublin to Tallaght only to find that their leadership was relying more upon patriotic zeal than an actual battle plan. And, as things turned out, there was no popular uprising in Dublin after all. The next day the Irish Constabulary and the British Army began the task of hunting down young Fenians throughout the hills south of Dublin. It was a task they pursued with efficiency and enthusiasm.

In the following weeks, newspapers featured daily lists of men, both Protestant and Catholic, arrested and headed for prison. The residence of a certain Edward Hanlon was listed as 24 Wexford St., the address of one of the Murphy candy shops. Joseph was fortunate enough to escape arrest, but, as he told his sons years later, his name was discovered on a list of rebels, who, if found, would be executed. He slipped out of Dublin, went into hiding, and avoided the authorities until he was able to book steerage passage for America. He arrived at Castle Garden on the southern tip of Manhattan in 1870.

Castle Garden was an old fort converted into an entry point for immigrants 15 years earlier. Its secure walls were intended to protect them from the bands of thieves, confidence men, and abductors who roamed New York's docks, preying on the new

Castle Garden, 1868. Photo courtesy of the Library of Congress.

arrivals. Eight million immigrants passed through Castle Garden until Ellis Island opened in 1892.

Fragments of his first days in America survive in stories Joseph told his family over the years. It's possible that some have ripened with age. He said that after passing through emigration, he lacked money for a carriage so he wrapped a few items in a shirt, pushed his trunk into the harbor, and walked to a nearby boarding house. He recalled rooms heated by only a single pipe running through the walls and across the ceiling. There was the story of how he was so absorbed watching workmen build the Brooklyn Bridge that he poured salt into the cup of coffee he bought with his last nickel.

One of the items he pulled from his trunk was a small, bronze crucifix that would make its way through the next three generations before being hung on my bedroom wall. On the backside of the cross is a Gaelic knot. At its top is a metal loop that could have been attached to a rosary or a cincture worn around the waist of a nun. Some secrets remain hidden forever, and there's no way of knowing if he received it as a parting gift from a friend, family member, or perhaps from a nun as a blessing for the voyage ahead and his new life in America. Nevertheless, it's the only surviving physical evidence of his passage.

America was the perfect place for a young man who, by nature, suffered fools poorly. He developed a pattern of holding a job only as long as his boss didn't try to tell him what to do. For the next few years, he bounced from city to city along the East Coast, working in lozenge and candy factories. As a boy in Dublin he had learned candy-making in the European traditions. Now he was learning how to work with American ingredients and machinery in large-scale factories with regimented labor.

His travels eventually took him to the Midwest. He was living in Chicago when he became a U.S. citizen on November 6, 1876.

Newlywed Margaret Switzer Murphy, early 1880s. Photo courtesy of the Murphy Family.

A rakish Frederick Michael Switzer, ca. 1885. Photo courtesy of Tom Switzer.

The first mention of him residing in St. Louis was in the 1879 City Directory, where his occupation was listed as "confectioner." No pattern in his life up to this time suggested that moving to St. Louis was any part of a greater plan. He found a job at the Dunham Coconut Factory as a candy maker, where he met a young woman named Margaret, who smashed coconuts with her younger brother Frederick. Joseph was 17 years older than Margaret. The women of Kerry Patch warned her to watch out, that the old man certainly had a wife back in Dublin. Such things were known to have happened. They were married on February 24, 1881, at the church of St. Lawrence O'Toole in Kerry Patch. Joseph was 34 and Margaret was 17.

The mother of Joseph's new bride was Margaret Morkin Switzer. She had raised her children in St. Louis's rough and tumble Irish slum after her husband Michael had drowned some years earlier, falling off a boat he had been unloading on the landing.

On a personal note, several years ago I visited Dublin to see these places I'd heard so much about. I wanted to walk through the streets, breathe the air, maybe even touch the doors of the shops where my family had lived and worked. I visited Glasnevin Cemetery and found Bernard Murphy's grave. One-hundred-fifty years of Irish weather had worn his stone down to a small lump.

I had a hunch that the Murphys had been parishioners of St. Mary's Pro-Cathedral on Marlborough Street. Completed in 1825, it was an imposing structure and an easy walk from Capel Street. The parish office was open so I dropped in and asked the sister at the desk if a Joseph Bernard Murphy was baptized there. She disappeared for a short while and returned with a document certifying that the sacrament had been performed on June 20, 1847. I asked her if the baptismal font in the cathedral was the same that would have been there that day. She said that indeed it was, though she seemed to think it a peculiar question, since Irish baptismal fonts so rarely need updating.

With the document in my hand, I stood at the very place where Bernard and Catherine Murphy had their son baptized. Illuminated by candles and a dim glow from the stained-glass windows, there was nothing in that immense, holy space to offer a clue as to what day or what century it might have been. It was perfectly quiet, with no sound or movement to distract from the moment or restrain my imagination from traveling through time. It was as if I could see them with their baby and the priest and the two witnesses named on the certificate. It was as if a curtain had slipped back, revealing that moment on a spring day in 1847 in a way that let me feel their real presence.

The sensation lasted less than a minute, but I felt I had experienced a moment of magic, an instant transcending time and continents, when the Old World had touched the New.

St. Louis's riverfront at the turn of the 20th century, the site
of four Switzer's factories between 1886 and 1977.
Photo courtesy of Library of Congress.

CHAPTER TWO

Kerry Patch

St. Louis in the 1880s seemed destined to become one of America's great cities. By the end of the decade it was the fourth largest in the country. Completion of the Eads Bridge in 1874 connected St. Louis to the eastern United States by rail, marking the decline of the steamboat era while opening new markets for its expanding manufacturing base. Factories and warehouses lined the blocks along its riverfront.

The city was rising up in red brick. It was common for new construction sites to have their own freshly dug clay pits and kilns to shape and fire bricks on site. The edges of the city were reserved for the wealthy, while the city's poor residents, who were largely foreign-born, lived in tightly packed slums where the air was heavy with coal smoke and putrid fumes from animal rendering plants. Industrial waste and sewage discharged into the sewers, fouling the river and the city's water supply.

St. Louis's riverfront with Eads Bridge, ca. 1900. Photo courtesy of Missouri History Museum, St. Louis.

The immigrant population, particularly Irish and German, had grown steadily since the 1840s, but the degree and nature of Irish poverty seemed worthy of particular disgust among many native-born St. Louisans. Cartoons in local newspapers depicted them as apes. "Irish and Catholics Need Not Apply" was a common message on factory gates, shop windows, and in "Help Wanted" ads in the daily newspapers. Still fresh in the minds of many St. Louisans was the riot of 1854 when a nativist mob ran riot for three days. A burst of xenophobic violence destroyed more than 100 homes and businesses in an Irish neighborhood near the levee, killing 10 of its residents.

After their marriage, Joseph and Margaret Murphy moved into a flat in Kerry Patch. It was important to Margaret that they live within easy walking distance of the small house where her mother, her sister Mary Ellen, and her brother Fred lived. There was no other neighborhood where working class Irish were welcome and, even if there had been, it wouldn't have occurred to them to live anywhere that was not Irish and Roman Catholic.

The first residents of Kerry Patch were a group of immigrants arriving from County Kerry in the 1840s. They heard there was undeveloped land just north of downtown that belonged to a wealthy Irish family, the Mullanphys. Many of the newcomers moved in as squatters, but the Mullanphys had done well in St. Louis and were glad to share their good fortune with their countrymen.

St. Louis's earliest Irish immigrants moved comfortably through the city's business, political, and cultural circles. It didn't hurt that many of them were Protestant. That changed as famine and political unrest drove larger numbers of Irish Catholics to rapidly growing American cities like St. Louis. As nativist groups like the Know Nothing Party and the American Protective Association poisoned public opinion against them, unemployment rose and living conditions deteriorated.

An 1878 St. Louis city guide described its Irish population as "poor but independent ... whose chief amusements consist of punching each other's eyes." Within Kerry Patch, slums within the slum had their own names like Poverty Pocket, Battle Row, Wild Cat Chute, and Castle Thunder. Gangs, often with political ties to City Hall, ruled their own small territories.

One of the more charitable descriptions of St. Louis's Irish at the time appeared in a *Post-Dispatch* article on May 13, 1888, describing Kerry Patch as a neighborhood:

" ... peopled by a race, whose faults are for the most part based on the impulsive and fed by the hot blood, which centuries of semi-bondage have but served to quicken, and whose virtues are of the heart and not of the head."

Conditions in Kerry Patch were so deplorable that the Civic League, in its 1907 Housing Reform Report, included photographs of street scenes in the neighborhood to frighten wealthy St. Louisans into donating to private model tenements, an early form of assisted housing. Progressive St. Louisans, with some support from the well-heeled, succeeded in building one such tenement, which they named the Mullanphy House, in honor of the wealthy Irish benefactors. However, it soon became clear that the problem would not be solved by building one tenement at a time. Popular sentiment at the time didn't favor spending public money to solve social problems on the scale of Kerry Patch.

St. Lawrence O'Toole and St. Bridget of Erin Catholic Churches offered what relief they could, but the citizens of Kerry Patch needed jobs. The young men of the neighborhood would eventually find paths to the middle class by joining the police and fire departments or rising through ward politics. In the meantime, the Near North Side remained a patch of Irish poverty until World War I, when Eastern European and African-American arrivals to the city took the places of the Irish in the same derelict blocks. Years later it would be the site of

Drawing of Kerry Patch, 1875. Photo courtesy of Compton and Dry's Pictorial St. Louis.

the Carr Square Village and Pruitt-Igoe housing projects. It would remain a landscape of vacant lots and shells of buildings into the twenty-first century.

Joseph and Margaret Murphy's second oldest son, Fred, was born in the Patch in 1887 and was fond, as an older man, of telling stories about growing up there. It was, he said, a neighborhood surrounded by other neighborhoods, all caught in their own desperate straits.

"They were rough days, there in the Patch" he remembered. "If we got up in North St. Louis and got in among the Poles, nobody knew us; then we were in trouble. If we went below Market Street into the German neighborhood, we got in trouble. If they came above Market Street into Kerry Patch, they got in trouble."

Fred Murphy was fond of telling a story about his uncle Fred Switzer that, even if it never happened, has become a matter of fact among the Murphy side of the family. It's the tale of how Fred had been harangued long enough by his neighbors who did not believe that Switzer was an Irish name. Pushed to the breaking point, he walked south of Market to the German parish there and told the pastor he was looking for a place to live. The priest, who saw through Switzer's plan, was outraged. "You would leave your mother and your sisters in that godforsaken place so that you can save your own sorry self? Shame on you. You will return there this very minute." Switzer was indeed ashamed and asked the priest if he would accompany him. "I will," replied Father, as he reached for his hat. "As far as Market Street."

Joseph, Margaret, and her young brother Frederick knew that the only opportunities they would ever see would be ones they created for themselves. All three had experience in the candy business. Joseph knew how to make it. Margaret knew the retail side from selling it in her mother's grocery store. Fred had spent much of his boyhood peddling it on the streets of Kerry Patch and the riverfront.

They chipped in to buy the ingredients they needed to make penny candies, and Joe cooked them in the oven in his flat. Fred sold them throughout the neighborhood from a wicker basket. There is no record of who came up with this business plan, but it was most likely the practically minded Margaret. She would have seen the sense in linking the street-smart drive of her 16-year-old brother with her husband's candy-making talents to devise a plan that would free them from Kerry Patch.

While Joseph turned her kitchen into a factory and her brother Fred roamed the streets hawking their wares, Margaret gave birth to a daughter. She named her Kate, but her life was not to be a long one. Kate died on March 7, 1884, two months short of her second birthday. The loss of an infant was not unusual in Kerry Patch, but that was little comfort to Margaret or her husband.

Joseph Murphy had experienced his own share of hardship, but the Switzers had grown up in harder times than he could have known. Young Frederick quit school when he was nine. In the winter he walked along the railroad tracks, gathering coal that had spilled off the trains to fuel the small stove that heated their home. His sisters, Margaret and Mary Ellen, were fiercely protective of their young brother. And though the Switzers were known to fuss among each other, they shared an unbreakable loyalty that grew over the years into an exclusive bond that would endure as long as they lived.

Murphy the candy maker and Switzer the salesman developed a successful partnership, and by 1884 they had established a legally registered company, Murphy and Switzer Candy. Two years later they moved production from the kitchen into a five-story brick building at 11 N. Main St. (known in later years as First Street). If it were still standing today, it would sit directly between the legs of the Gateway Arch, but in the mid-1800s, Main was a narrow, cobblestone street, lined block after block with brick warehouses and factories, many built after the Great Fire of 1849. Constructed in 1851, the Murphy and Switzer factory had a row of wide double doors, making it easy to carry raw materials in from the street and load finished products onto wagons at the curb. Joseph Bernard Murphy was the president and Frederick Michael Switzer served as vice president. The company regularly ran newspaper ads requesting "first-class lozenge cutters," "caramel workers," "cream dippers," "chocolate dippers," and "girls for slab work."

They were producing the kinds of candy Joseph had learned to make at the shops and factories he'd worked in since he was a boy. Joseph was not a chemist, but he'd always had a special way with caramel. He knew instinctively how the various elements would combine to produce a range of tastes. A trick he learned in Dublin was to mix the candy with butter that had grown slightly rancid. He knew that if he boiled it and strained out the impurities, the taste of his caramels would have a more interesting edge. To him, it was an art.

The Murphy and Switzer Candy Company started with a small, generally unskilled group of employees. Working conditions were on par with the typical factory of the day. Workdays were long and six-day weeks were the norm. There were few safety precautions on the work floor, and the average wage for the men was a little over a dollar per day. The women earned less. Workers had no union and no voice in the operation of the plant. Candy had always been a seasonal business, so when sales slowed, the company laid off the employees. If workers had grievances, they were free to leave. In the early days, Murphy worked alongside the employees with his hand in every aspect of the candy-making process. He bought the ingredients, mixed and cooked the batches, and constantly experimented with new product ideas. Switzer was more interested in the long-term strategies of the company and how to market it.

Occasional items in the newspapers would mention the factory, usually shining a grim light on some unfortunate soul. A 16-year-old boy was arrested in December of 1892 for breaking open a bucket that had been sitting on the sidewalk in front of the plant and making off with a dollar's worth of candy. In November of 1893, Henry Stover, a 20-year-old worker, fell from an open window on the fifth floor to the street below. The *Globe-Democrat* speculated that "the poor fellow must have been killed instantly" and reported that his sister, Mary Stover, who also worked at the factory, told police she believed he had an epileptic seizure.

A photograph from that era captures the company's employees lined along the sidewalk in front of the factory. Everyone's eyes are fixed on the camera. The women stand together in the doorway. The men, spread out in front of the building, confidently rest

Murphy and Switzer Candy Company, late 1880s. Photo courtesy of the Murphy Family.

their hands on their hips. A couple of them, maybe salesmen, wear bowler hats and practice casual poses. There are several children among the workers. Standing in the doorway behind the employees are Frederick Switzer in a derby hat and Joseph Murphy, who at 5-foot-4 peeks out between two of the women.

Capturing this moment must have been important enough to stop the production line, a rare occurrence in any factory. Maybe the two partners believed that a photograph would stand as lasting proof that dreams really can be spun from candy. It's possible that the men and women who look at us from this photograph meant to show that their work had earned them a stake in this enterprise as well and that they, too, deserved to be remembered.

Neither Joe nor Fred had more than basic grade-school educations, so it is unlikely that either had heard the term "social Darwinism." Nevertheless, they would have had no trouble understanding it. Their world was a place inhabited by two kinds of people: Irish Catholics and everyone else. And it was a world from which they expected no favors. Opportunities existed for those willing to grab and hold onto them, and that required more strength than kindness. The candy factory was their only way out of poverty—a door opening to a world of acceptance and respect. It was their factory, and their survival depended upon its success. There was no place for anyone who stood in their way. They would be damned before they would return to poverty.

In many ways the two men were similar. Neither had known a father and each learned strength at an early age from determined, smart women who kept their families together by running small shops. But there were differences as well. In addition to being almost young enough to be Joe's son, Fred had more acute business skills, sharpened by a childhood of bargaining over pennies with tough customers in a rough neighborhood. Joe was more of a dreamer, creator, and rebel who was suspicious of authority.

Joseph Bernard Murphy, ca. 1880. Photo courtesy of the Murphy Family.

It is an Irish compliment to credit someone with the ability to tell a man to go to hell in a way that makes him look forward to the trip. Joseph Murphy could do that.

Margaret and Joseph would have more children in the coming years, all boys. Joe Jr. was born in 1884, followed by Fred in 1887, Bernard in 1890, and Francis in 1892.

The families were closely-knit in the years of the late 1880s and early '90s. Joseph and Margaret lived on North Jefferson Avenue, just a short walk from where Fred Switzer lived with his mother and older sister, Mary Ellen, on Division Street. The houses on Division were tiny brick cottages with tin roofs. The Switzers shared three rooms and a kitchen, heated by a coal stove. The city didn't provide water to Division Street, so gutters carried rainwater from the roof to a well in the back yard.

Young Fred Murphy, who was in grade school at the time, would visit his Switzer relatives almost daily. He remembered how the women of the family would dote upon his uncle Frederick, now in his mid-20s. His Grandma Morkin would make mashed potatoes that reminded him of little mountains, and sometimes she would grill some meat on the stove. She'd serve her son first and then split what he didn't eat among the rest. When Fred would get ready to head back home, his grandma would almost always give him a penny, sometimes a nickel, and sternly warn him with a wink, "Don't let the Old Maid see you with this," referring to Mary Ellen, who did not believe in spoiling children.

But the time for even such small indulgences was growing short.

The Panic of 1893 was a series of financial collapses, creating the worst economic depression the United States had ever experienced. More than 600 banks and 15,000 businesses failed that first year, and unemployment topped 20 percent. It took four years for the economy to recover fully, and St. Louis suffered along with the rest of the nation. There were heavy casualties among the city's manufacturers, including the Murphy and Switzer Candy Company.

The company faced bankruptcy early in the crisis. In late 1893, two brothers, Crawford and Charles Kendrick, took ownership of the candy plant from Murphy and Switzer, making it a part of an entity known as the Interstate Candy Company. The Kendricks were, as the *Post-Dispatch* described them, "very popular in St. Louis society and much sought after, both for their personal attractions, both being handsome, unmarried men, with polished manners and high educational advantages, and because they were believed to be quite wealthy."

So, it was quite a surprise when, in March of 1895, the Kendrick brothers skipped town in such haste that they left their luggage in their rooms. The *Post* described the mess as "a sensational state of affairs in commercial circles." It seems these charming fellows had been kiting money among several of their enterprises, including Interstate Candy and Murphy and Switzer. The house of cards had finally collapsed.

Mary Ellen Switzer, early 1880s. Photo courtesy of Tom Switzer.

It was big sister Mary Ellen Switzer who came to the rescue. Aunt Nellie, as she is commonly known by her Murphy descendants, is remembered in family legend as a dark and powerful force of nature. She left home when she was 18, without her mother's permission, to marry a man by the name of Martin Broderick.

Broderick was an agreeable fellow when sober, who sold and traded horses and mules throughout the West. After several years of adventures, Mary Ellen left him and moved back home to St. Louis as the prodigal daughter.

Fred Murphy remembered his aunt as intriguing and a little frightening. Years later he described her as a woman of mystery.

"It must have been during these times trading horses that she acquired the habits and tricks of both the Indians and Gypsies, particularly the reading of cards, tea leaves, reading palms, and telling fortunes. And believe me, she was tops in those things, with her black eyes, black hair, and her habit of looking clean through a person."

Frederick M. Switzer, ca. 1900. Photo courtesy of Tom Switzer.

In an effort to pull her younger brother from bankruptcy, Mary Ellen stepped into the shambles of what had been Murphy and Switzer. Sorting out the financial tangles of the Kendrick Brothers, she was able to acquire more than $11,000 of candy inventory for $2,000, which she had saved from her years of horse trading. She loaned it to her brother, who hauled the candy across the street to a vacant building at 22 N. Main, a warehouse owned by a friend. The company was renamed the M.E. Switzer Candy Company, and 30-year-old Frederick Michael Switzer was its president.

And so it was in the year of 1895 that Joseph B. Murphy, married to Fred's sister and father to four young boys, found himself no longer the head of a candy company and no longer employed.

St. Patrick's Day parade in Kerry Patch, 1874.
Photo courtesy of Missouri History Museum, St. Louis.

CHAPTER THREE

Family Matters

Joseph Murphy knew that as long as he could make candy, he would never have to worry about how he was going to make a living. He borrowed $500 from a friend in Chicago and rented a small commercial space several blocks from the river on Pine Street where he made crystallized bonbons. But without the benefit of his brother-in-law's marketing know-how, the business barely lasted a year. "He just wasn't a merchant," conceded his son Fred.

In 1896, he packed up the family and moved to Winthrop, Massachusetts, where he got a job making a sweet lozenge for the Chase Candy Company. It was a good opportunity. Chase was in the process of merging with other small candy makers to form the New England Candy Company, or NECCO, which would eventually manufacture a famous candy wafer of the same name.

It had been a rough couple of years, and Joseph was undoubtably glad to be out of Kerry Patch, out of bankruptcy, and once again fully engaged in the creative end of the candy business. The only reason he had ever remained in St. Louis was because of his wife's attachment to her family. He still valued, as he always had, the freedom to pull up stakes and head off for fresh horizons. He honored his responsibilities as a husband and a parent, but he wasn't comfortable with binding, personal commitments. He'd barely kept in touch with his family in Ireland. His mother had remarried, and they rarely corresponded. Two of his brothers moved to Liverpool. Another brother, Bernard, moved to St. Louis and worked as a candy maker, but they had little social contact. Joseph Murphy was a man who kept his baggage light.

The Murphys moved into a two-story wood-frame house on the beach. The spans of ocean and sky and the smells of salt and fish must have amazed Margaret and the four boys, none of whom had ever been outside St. Louis. Joseph had developed an interest in photography and bought a camera that created images on specially treated glass plates. He built a darkroom in his new home and roamed the beach and surrounding neighborhood taking pictures of his family. The glass plates exist to this day. Margaret, covered from head to toe in her swimsuit, smiles from a beached rowboat. The boys sit still long enough for a few group shots on the shore before, as we can imagine, they burst loose, chasing each other down the beach like monkeys.

But there were signs that this happy chapter would be brief. Shortly before they left St. Louis, Margaret Morkin née Switzer died at the age of 60. She had been the rock of the Switzer clan, the gravitational center of the family since her husband drowned 30 years earlier. Her children (Margaret, Mary Ellen, and Fred) had never been separated. And now Margaret was in Massachusetts, 1,500 miles away.

Meanwhile, Fred Switzer, operating out of the new plant at 22 N. Main, realized that he did not know how to make candy. In what must have been an uncomfortable mission, he took the train to Winthrop to ask his brother-in-law to return to St. Louis and rejoin the company. Joseph, the amateur photographer,

Margaret Switzer in Winthrop, Massachusetts, 1895. Photo courtesy of the Murphy Family.

Murphy boys, (left to right) Bernard, Fred, and Francis in Winthrop, 1895. Photo courtesy of the Murphy Family.

apparently saw enough importance and perhaps a touch of irony in the moment to ask Fred to pose with his boys in front of the house. Fred obliged, though grudgingly. We know this because the photograph of his humble pilgrimage is preserved to this day in both Murphy and Switzer family albums.

The meeting did not go well. Switzer offered to hire Murphy back as an employee. Murphy countered with a demand for a guaranteed 12 months of work, regardless of the seasonal demands for candy. Switzer refused, Murphy turned him down, and Switzer went home.

Fred Switzer visits the Murphys in Winthrop, 1896. Photo courtesy of the Murphy Family.

Conversations at the Murphy house must have been tense over the following months. Joseph was adamant about not taking a deal that he found insulting. He was the candy man. To his thinking, it was his confectionery creations that people loved. The company he had started in his own kitchen had been snatched from him by a conspiring brother-in-law and his horse-trading sister. His wife saw it differently. From her perspective as a Switzer, Mary Ellen had ensured a future for the candy business, and why shouldn't their brother lead it? As a Murphy by marriage, she was certain that her brother Fred was not the marrying type and that someday the company would pass to her sons. Such a plan hinged on Joseph returning to the company and preparing the way for his progeny.

They had barely settled into their new home by the sea when Murphy, forever restless, moved the family to Nashville, where he had found a job with the National Biscuit Company. Homesick and increasingly less certain that her husband would ever settle down, Margaret insisted that he bring them all back to St. Louis so she could rejoin her siblings. He did, briefly, then left unexpectedly, by himself, for San Francisco after hearing that there were opportunities there for a good candy man.

After a short time, Margaret received a letter from her husband informing her that he had received an offer to work in Hawaii. Margaret responded that he would do so "over her dead body." That wasn't necessary. Margaret could be persuasive when pushed past a point, and Joseph returned to St. Louis in 1898 to rejoin his family; however, when it came to working at her brother's candy company, he would not budge.

Without the skills to create new and original candy products, Switzer purchased formulas and finished penny candies from other companies. He formed a corporation called the Missouri Candy Company as an umbrella over several divisions that made and sold different brands of candy. In order to create an air of importance around some of his more popular products, he would often give them their own company names. For example, he dubbed his chewing gum operation the Missouri Gum Company.

Fred was developing a reputation in the candy business as an impressive young figure on the rise. The July 1900 edition of the *Confectioners' and Bakers' Gazette* took note of his presence at the National Confectioners' Association convention at Niagara Falls as he meandered among the crowd, dispensing samples of his latest chewing gum:

"F.M. Switzer, of the Missouri Gum Company . . . was the coolest looking man in the convention. No amount of running around could mar the air of general coolness and ease that graced his shoulders like a mantle."

Meanwhile, Switzer was looking for a product that would put his company on the map, something the public would identify as *the* Switzer candy. If he couldn't create it himself, he would buy it. He didn't need to look far. Another St. Louis entrepreneur, appropriately named Walter W. Candy, had recently founded a company called Busy Bee Candy. Switzer bought Busy Bee's formula for a honey-flavored candy kiss called the Yellow Jacket. The Yellow Jacket became an immediate hit, prompting Switzer to turn it into his flagship product. The legal name of the overall operation would continue to be the Missouri Candy Company; it would manufacture a variety of candies, but it would do business as Switzer's Yellow Jacket Company for the next 40 years.

Fred Switzer might not have had Joe Murphy's talent for making candy, but his business and marketing instincts were equal to anyone's. Few men, for example, would have seen the opportunity to use a streetcar strike to promote candy, but Fred Switzer did.

Yellow Jackets, a candy worth renaming the company. Photo courtesy of the Switzer's Licorice Archive.

On May 9, 1900, over 3,000 St. Louis streetcar workers went on strike in an attempt to organize themselves as a local within the Amalgamated Street Railway Employees of America. The previous year, 10 local streetcar lines had consolidated into two, leaving workers no bargaining power. They demanded shorter workdays, better pay, and safer working conditions. The larger of the two companies, the St. Louis Transit Company, fired more than 3,000 of its employees. The St. Louis

Kerry Patch at 15th and O'Fallon Streets during the streetcar strike, 1900. Photo courtesy of Missouri History Museum, St. Louis by photographer J. Edward Roesch.

police reassigned 1,000 of its officers to operate the lines and deputized 2,500 civilians as a strike-breaking posse.

On the first day all hell broke loose across the city as strikers and their sympathizers tore up tracks, lit fires, threw trash over the wires, and piled rocks on the tracks to halt service. Women from the Garment Workers Union lined up across Washington as a human blockade. The strike highlighted class differences across the city. Thirteen-year-old Fred Murphy, back from the beach at Winthrop, was part of more than one rock-throwing crowd as streetcars tried to pass through Kerry Patch. Seventy years later, he recalled being chased through the alleys by police, who were never quite fast enough to catch him.

There were several incidents of posse members firing their weapons into crowds, killing and injuring strikers, demonstrators, and bystanders. Strikers were no less reluctant to use violence to achieve their own ends. Police foiled three attempts to dynamite the barracks of temporary workers.

There was little else on anyone's mind as the turmoil from the strike stretched through a hot St. Louis summer. One article in the *Post-Dispatch* on July 29 was particularly interesting. It was hard to miss, positioned beneath a drawing of seven young women and a large, bold headline proclaiming: "Pretty Chewing Gum Girls Form a Union."

The story reported that 35 "girls" employed by Switzer's Yellow Jacket Company had obtained a charter from the Central Trades and Labor Union for a chewing gum workers union. They had elected officers, and most of the article focused on the young leader of their local.

The *Post* reported that, "Miss Mary Mausehund, the president of the new organization, is an unusually attractive young woman, 19 years old, who lives with her widowed mother at 3631 Dodier. She is rather below the medium height, is plump, but not stout and is of a happy disposition.

"She has jet black hair, a full round face, and large white teeth that show behind a rather large and well-formed mouth. Her eyes are large and black, and are full of life. They sparkle when she talks, and are full of intelligence."

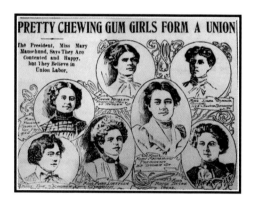

Headline declaring Switzer's first labor union, 1900. Photo courtesy of the St. Louis Post-Dispatch.

The story eventually exhausted the subject of her personal appearance and got around to her thoughts on organized labor. Miss Mausehund, who had worked since she was 12, had just recently been inspired to organize the gum wrappers.

"We never thought of organizing the union until the big streetcar strike came on. The noble fight that the streetcar men were making aroused our admiration and excited our sympathy," she told the paper in a statement impressively and suspiciously articulate for a young woman with less than a sixth-grade education.

She described their work as taking cakes of gum, wrapping them in small pieces of paper, and putting them in boxes. For that, they were paid $1.00 to $1.25 per day. And lest there be any misunderstanding, she assured readers that the gum wrapper girls had no intention of organizing their own strike.

"We don't want more wages or shorter hours. We think we have a pretty good thing as it now stands, and we want to keep it that way. All we want is to keep the business up to its present standard."

The article reported, "F.M. Switzer, the president of the company employing the girls, is heartily in sympathy with their movement, and he assisted them in their organization."

What more could a girl want? "Mr. Switzer heartily approved our plan and he has had labels printed showing that our goods are strictly union made and packed," Miss Mausehund confirmed.

And though it seemed out of character for Frederick Switzer to publicly declare his support for organized labor, every piece of gum issuing forth from Switzer's Yellow Jacket Company would proclaim in print its solidarity with the working men and women of St. Louis. It seemed the right thing to do at the dawn of a new century, and it didn't hurt sales.

By September the strike was over. Workers found themselves quite literally outgunned by the armed company enforcers. In the end they achieved no gains in pay or working conditions. Fourteen people were dead and 200 wounded, with extensive property damage in neighborhoods throughout the city.

Meanwhile, Margaret was doing her best to bridge divisions in the family. She was determined to bring her husband back into

Buttermels, a caramel candy with Irish roots. Photo courtesy of the Switzer's Licorice Archive.

the company, but her arguments fell on deaf ears. It should have been easy. Joe was restless and looking for opportunities to create new candies and Fred wanted to expand the product line. Unfortunately, neither man would take the first step. Eventually, an opportunity presented itself.

Switzer heard that the Woodward Candy Company in Council Bluffs, Iowa, was producing a butter caramel that was selling very well. He asked Joe, with whom he was apparently still on speaking terms, if he could design a similar product. Joe was initially reluctant, because caramels didn't hold up in the hot St. Louis summers, and he wouldn't take a job that didn't guarantee 12 months of work. He countered with his own proposal. If he invented a caramel that could withstand the heat and humidity of the summer months, Switzer would be obliged to hire him as the head of production with guaranteed year-round employment. Switzer agreed, and Murphy got to work creating a new product.

If "sugar-whisperer" were a vocation, Joseph Murphy would have held that title. He had an uncanny way of working with sugar at a time when suppliers offered little consistency in quality. He could take a refined sugar, a Cuban sugar, a brown sugar, or whatever was available and turn out the same product day after day. After some tinkering, he created a candy called the Buttermel. Its success lay in its predictable taste and its ability to hold up in most weather. Advertisements in papers across the country described the Buttermel as "different from any candy, not a butterscotch and not a caramel—but a delightful combination of the good in both. It can't be beat!" It remained a star in the Switzer product line for decades, eventually outselling the Yellow Jacket. The century had barely begun, and the partnership was back in operation with the egos of both men intact.

Reunited. Joe Murphy (sitting) with Fred Switzer. Photo courtesy of Tom Switzer.

It was a time of rapid growth in the American candy industry. As sugar processing and refining techniques developed, the cost of the candy's primary ingredient plummeted, turning it from a luxury item into a product anyone, even a child, could buy on an impulse. Between the turn of the century and World War I, producers of candy, from large factories to small specialty confectioneries, doubled in St. Louis to about 100 companies.

The competition came from all sides and in every shape and size. The National Candy Company was a candy-making behemoth. Founded in the first decade of the century by Vincent Leonard Price Sr., father of the famous horror film actor, National operated a couple of dozen factories with its headquarters in St. Louis. It was best known for its jellybeans and jawbreakers.

Charles Frederick Wenneker, president of the candy giant Blanke-Wenneker, got into the candy business when he was a teenager. By 1912, he was claiming that his factory on Market Street was the biggest candy manufacturer in the West. He was also a crafty marketer, including a coupon in every box of chocolate that year that one could mail in and receive an engraving of the Titanic "as a souvenir of one of the greatest tragedies of the century."

John Mavrakos moved to St. Louis from Greece in 1904, and by 1913 he had opened an ice cream parlor where he also sold homemade candies from his family's recipes. They were so popular that he opened a chain of stores throughout the area.

Though they couldn't have known it at the time, some of these mom-and-pop operations would evolve into national candy dynasties. Frank Mars, who learned how to hand dip chocolates as a youngster, began making candy in his family's kitchen in 1911. Three generations later, the Mars clan would be the third richest family in America.

Milton Hershey learned to make candy as an apprentice at a small confectionery in Lancaster, Pennsylvania. After learning the trade, he went out on his own and developed a tasty caramel. But when he saw his first candy-making machinery at the 1893 Chicago World's Fair, he sold the caramel company and turned his attention to chocolate. Hershey implemented the first production techniques to turn out a nickel candy bar faster and cheaper. He was fond of saying, "Caramels are just a fad, but chocolate is a permanent thing."

David L. Clark, also an Irish immigrant, took technical innovations in candy production even further when he invented

Buttermels display box, ca. 1920. Photo courtesy of Switzer's Licorice Archive.

his eponymous candy bar in 1917. The Clark Bar incorporated a thin milk chocolate shell around a filling of ground peanuts with a caramel core. It was the first so-called "combination" candy bar, small and individually wrapped to make it easy to send to American troops fighting in France. It caught on immediately and inspired other candy makers to experiment with their own combinations.

Fred Switzer was well aware of the competition and understood that if his business was to grow, it would have to become more than just a brick and mortar factory that made candy. While it was best known to the public for its Yellow Jackets, Switzer's Missouri Candy Company was hard at work developing other sources of profit and growth.

Candy jobber peddling Switzer's Buttermels, ca. 1910. Photo courtesy of Switzer's Licorice Archive.

Long before the days of sophisticated, far-reaching distribution systems, candy moved from factories to consumers through independent operators called "jobbers," who bought the candy from manufacturers at reduced prices and then marked it up, carted it around town on horse-drawn wagons, and sold it to retailers. Switzer negotiated a deal with the top 10 jobbing

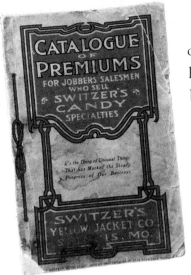

1912 edition of Switzer's Catalogue of Premiums, offering incentives to salesmen. Photo courtesy of Missouri History Museum, St. Louis.

operations in the city. He would offer them his own candy along with products he bought from his competitors.

By cornering what came be known as the "Big Ten," he developed an early distribution system, earning bigger profits by moving larger volumes of candy more efficiently with reduced costs. The business grew even larger when he began buying and selling sugar, molasses, and other raw materials for making candy. "You've got to give the devil his due," said his nephew Fred Murphy. "The man succeeded at everything he touched. But Lord help you if you were ever on the other end of the deal. You ran into a ripsaw."

As national networks of wholesale distribution developed during the early years of the new century, Switzer's candy appeared in newspaper and magazine advertisements for grocery companies, candy shops, and department stores across the country. To inspire jobbers and salesmen, Switzer developed a national incentive system so they could earn prizes by selling his candy. *The Catalogue of Premiums for Jobbers Salesmen Who Sell Switzer's Candy Specialties* offered more than 100 pages of items, including jewelry, furniture, guns, vacuum cleaners, buggies, and bicycles. The more cases of Switzer's candy a salesman could sell, the more valuable a premium he would earn. The catalogue also included words of wisdom, such as "A Taste is Worth an Hour of Talk."

Fred had another motivation to succeed, which was at least as powerful as achieving the American Dream. That was paying back his sister, Mary Ellen, her $2,000. Again, we borrow from the memory of Fred Murphy, who was a teenager at the turn of the century and remembered doing odd jobs for his uncle at the factory at 22 N. Main:

> I can remember when I was a boy, and we'd see Aunt Nellie coming down the street. We knew and Switzer knew that she was coming down for some money. We'd pass the word to Switzer and he'd go down to the basement, and instead of coming out of the front of the building on Main Street, he'd go out the back on Commercial Alley and go down to Herbst Brothers Saloon on Walnut and First until Aunt Nellie had left the place. But he did pay her back, over and over again. She got her money; you can gamble on that.

Mature Mary Ellen Switzer, ca. 1910. Photo courtesy of Tom Switzer.

Any hard feelings the two partners had harbored after the breakup of Murphy and Switzer had since healed. Fred actually moved in with the Murphys for a while at their home on Easton Avenue. It seemed their early struggles were paying off. Margaret had her husband, her brother, and her four boys under one roof in a middle-class neighborhood several blocks west of Kerry Patch. They were preparing to move the factory from the old building at 22 N. Main St. to a larger plant at 806 N. Main, three blocks north of the Eads Bridge.

The early years of the new century seemed to smile on St. Louis. It was the fourth largest city in the nation, and plans were underway to celebrate the 100th anniversary of the Louisiana Purchase in Forest Park, where there would certainly be opportunities to sell candy. In 1904, Joseph was 57 years old and his sons ranged in age from 12 to 20. His partner Fred, at 39, was growing into a man of some promise, though he seemed to be a confirmed bachelor, fond of the pleasures of the city's night life. He was a regular at Tony Faust's elegant restaurant on Broadway and Elm, the acknowledged place to see and be seen.

"Those were the days of horse and buggies," recalled his nephew Fred Murphy. "He was a pretty good two-fisted drinker back then, and he had an educated horse. He'd get through drinking, and they'd put him in the buggy, put the reins down on the dashboard, and the horse would go back to the livery stable, and then the livery stable people would bring him back to our door."

He surprised them all when he married Elizabeth Kern on March 4, 1905. Bess would spend much of her married life smoothing out Fred's rougher edges and ensuring that he presented himself well to St. Louis society. And even though Mary Ellen and Margaret conceded that the Kerns were a step above the Switzers on St. Louis's social ladder, they were never convinced that she was quite good enough for their brother.

None of them could have known that they had unwittingly set into motion a chain of events that would produce three generations of Murphys and Switzers working together in a factory by the Eads Bridge.

CHAPTER FOUR

Factory by the Bridge

Murphy continued to create new products, and Switzer successfully marketed them. There was the Betterscotch, a follow up to the Buttermel. The Chocolate Soldier was touted for its ability to stand up to St. Louis summers "like a soldier" in an age of primitive refrigeration. Cocotels, a bite-sized coconut-flavored candy, came later. Orangels were a chewy gumdrop, Silk Creams, a creamy taffy, and the Delmar cream, a chocolate-covered cream bite.

The Chocolate Soldier, a candy undaunted by St. Louis summers. Photo courtesy of Swizter's Licorice Archive.

But a certain tension never left the relationship. Murphy jealously guarded his recipes. He suspected that if his partner knew the tricks behind the magic, he would look for ways to change the formulas to trim costs and sacrifice the quality. There is a moment that lives on in family legend when Joseph positioned himself squarely in the stairwell to the second floor, declaring that "no Switzer shall pass this point!"

A case of Betterscotch. Photo courtesy of Switzer's Licorice Archive.

Murphy had never been comfortable working for a salary or, for that matter, being employed by anyone. Particularly not by his younger brother-in-law, who was paying him twenty-five dollars a week. To make the point clear, he built a steamer trunk in the basement of the

22 N. Main, home of the Switzer Candy Company, ca. 1908. Photo courtesy of Switzer's Licorice Archive.

candy factory and announced in June of 1909 that he was returning to Ireland for a three-month visit. It was to be his first trip back since arriving in the United States almost 40 years earlier.

It was a surprising announcement, considering that Ireland was still under British occupation, and he was still a fugitive from his Fenian days. But it wasn't out of character for Joseph Murphy to shake the dust from his feet and seek a change of scenery. It's impossible to know if he was more motivated to visit family in Ireland or get away from family in St. Louis. He might have thought it was high time, after several years of domestic life, to have another adventure. Or maybe it occurred to him that at 62 years old, he had the right to do whatever he damn well pleased. His children were almost grown and his wife had shown herself countless times to be capable of handling whatever came her way. Fred Switzer and his growing family lived just down the block from the Murphys' new home on Cote Brilliante Avenue in the city's West End, so he could keep an eye on family and business matters.

It's also highly likely that he didn't give the whole matter much thought at all and just forged ahead.

The year 1909 was full of surprises. Shortly after returning from his trip abroad, Joseph moved the family again, but this time beyond the city's borders to the suburb of Webster Groves. Over the past several decades, a ring of small cities had grown around St. Louis, connected to the central city by a network of trains and trolleys. For those able to afford a house in one of these suburbs, it was possible to live in

Joseph B. Murphy ca. 1909. Photo courtesy of the Murphy Family.

a pastoral setting and commute easily to just about anywhere.

Edward Joy, an early developer in the area, was furiously buying land and building houses, and the Murphys bought one of his properties on Lockwood Avenue within an easy walk of the Old Orchard Frisco station. Fred Murphy, who was 22 at the time, recalled that there really was an orchard in Old Orchard and a genuine lake near Lake Avenue. The air was clean and the streets uncluttered with traffic. A few years later, Fred Switzer and his family would move to a house in Kirkwood at the corner of Argonne and Woodbine, the present site of Grace Episcopal Church.

The Murphys and the Switzers had made their way from Shanty to Lace Curtain Irish. The Murphys would be comfortable and middle class. The Switzers, though, were on their way to wealth and social position. From 1906 to 1916, Fred and Bess Switzer would have five sons and three daughters. Their children would eventually marry into prominent families and assume

Bess Switzer with her children, 1915. Photo courtesy of Tom Switzer.

respected positions in St. Louis business and society. The Murphys and the Switzers were still related by marriage, and they would continue to build a candy business together. But not as equals.

On July 29, 1910, this headline appeared in the *Globe-Democrat's* business section:

CANDY COMPANY TO MOVE
BUYS FIVE-STORY BUILDING ON
NORTH MAIN STREET
FOR $47,000

It was a move that would establish the company as a St. Louis landmark. The new factory's floor space was more than 60,000 square feet, twice the size of the building they had most recently occupied. All of their prior factories had been on Main Street, and this one was as well. But the new plant at 612 N. Main St. was adjacent to the Eads Bridge, and its southern wall offered a huge space for advertising their products over the next six decades. No one entering or leaving St. Louis by foot, train, streetcar, horse-drawn wagon, or automobile over the bridge could miss that huge sign.

Constructed in 1874, the factory was a formidable red brick building. A story-high cast-iron facade with fluted columns ran along its entire front wall on Main Street. It was modern for its day, with rows of tall windows along every floor, letting in a generous amount of light, along with the noise and soot of the city. Thick walls, tall ceilings, and heavy oak beams made it the perfect structure to support heavy industry. Its original owner was the Excelsior Manufacturing Company, which made cast-iron stoves. From the windows on its east wall, workers could view a constant flow of trains on the elevated tracks along Wharf Street. More trains rumbled past its south wall below the roadway of the Eads Bridge. In 1911, a row of boats would still be moored to the levee, less than a block down Washington Avenue.

Over the following year, Switzer's would invest yet another $13,000 in improvements and renovations—an enormous sum for the time. Years later, Joseph's son Fred would

Drawing of the Switzer Building as it appeared in 1875. Photo courtesy of Compton and Dry's Pictorial St. Louis.

recall that "The Old Gent," as he called his father, did a lot of the construction himself.

> I remember he ran in all the pipes for the steam work and the electrical work. In those days they didn't have inspectors like they do today. You could pay them a few bucks and everything would be fine. They used to have coal furnaces in the back, along Commercial Alley, and he ran all that pipe himself.

The new factory allowed production of a wider range of products, some invented by Murphy, others purchased from competitors. Shortly after moving into its new factory, the company added a product to its line that was unlike anything they'd made before. Black licorice was becoming a common sight in neighborhood candy stores across the country as it enjoyed an uptick in popularity. Several large companies, including the National Licorice Company in Brooklyn, were producing licorice penny candy molded into a variety of novel shapes.

Women of Switzer's Licorice Department, ca. 1920. Photo courtesy of Switzer's Licorice Archive.

Switzer's bought the Gem City Licorice Company in Dayton, Ohio, in 1912 and moved its licorice-making machinery to its St. Louis plant. In addition to gum, chocolate, taffy, caramel, and cream candies, Switzer's now had a brand-new assortment of licorice products. There was a small stick of licorice called The Popular and thin licorice ropes called Jumbo Twists. Licorice cigarettes, pipes, and cigars were especially popular among the younger set.

Fred Switzer began labeling his new candy as products of "Switzer's Licorice Company." He designed a special letterhead depicting the factory adorned with large "Switzer Licorice Co." signs. Although the factory actually had a large "Home of Buttermels" sign on its south wall, his new licorice division certainly deserved the rank of a full-fledged company. At least on a letterhead.

In the meantime, Joseph and Margaret's four sons had grown up. It had always been Margaret's hope that they would someday inherit the company, but that was a dim dream now. Still, the business was in their blood as they grew up working odd jobs in their family's factories. Candy had always been at the center of family life, the topic of dinner conversations, and the center of their world.

Joseph took satisfaction in his sons. They were living proof that his move to America was the right decision. He knew that life would be easier for them than it had been for him. They were first-generation Americans. They spoke without a brogue and had earned high school diplomas from the Christian Brothers. The stigmas of being Irish and Catholic in America were fading. His boys had grown up in a different world, and as far as he was concerned, they were free to do with their lives whatever they pleased. As he himself had always done.

Joe Jr. was the oldest. Handsome, hot tempered, and impetuous, he had inherited the black hair and eyes of his Grandmother Morkin and the restless spirit of his father. Joe was never particularly interested in working at the candy company, so he moved to Chicago to sell chewing gum for the Wrigley Company. That didn't last long, though. His uncle Frederick had developed a chewing gum he called Mint Leaf and persuaded Joe Jr. to return to St. Louis and sell it for him. Joe accepted, but it did not go well.

Apparently, Fred had not told Joe the entire story. The essential ingredient to chewing gum is chicle, a natural gum extracted from a tree in Mexico. Unfortunately, bad weather in Mexico, skyrocketing prices, and a dispute between Switzer and the American Chiclet company, which controlled

Murphy Family, 1910. Standing from left to right: Francis and Fred. Sitting: Joe Jr., Joseph Sr., Margaret, Bernard. Photo courtesy of the Murphy Family.

the supply of chicle, led Switzer to try coal tar as a substitute. Joe Jr.'s brother Fred recalled years later that Mint Leaf had a good taste. For about a minute. "When you had a lot of sugar and flavor at the beginning it was all right. After that, it tasted like you were chewing somebody's old socks," he said.

When Joe realized what he was selling, he was furious. He quit, and that was the end of Joe Jr. and Switzer's Yellow Jacket Company.

Joe's life was not a lucky one. In the winter of 1919, his wife Josephine complained of nausea and weakness. She did not know that she was pregnant with their first child. Committed to a flu ward, she and her unborn baby contracted Spanish Flu and died.

Tragedy, however, did not diminish his charm. Joe is remembered most from the stories he was known to tell at the drop of a hat. "Long ago in Ireland," he would spin. "There were monkeys living in the forests. And some of those monkeys fell out of the trees and came to America. And that's where the Murphys came from." It's a story told to young Murphys to this day.

Fred Murphy was three years younger than his brother Joe and had his own set of problems working at the factory. He tried it for a while before the World War and for a short time afterward, but he continuously argued with his father and his uncle over the nine dollars per week that they paid him. When he complained to his mother Margaret about how stingy Switzer was, he said, "She'd be all over me. That was her brother, and nobody could talk about a Switzer like that." It was only a matter of time before Switzer fired him and he moved to Atlanta, where he spent the rest of his career working in the candy business with considerably less drama.

In spite of their bickering, Fred and his uncle shared one particular adventure that was reported in the *St. Louis Globe-Democrat*. In 1912, Switzer purchased an automobile, and Fred occasionally served as his chauffeur. On a Sunday evening in March, as they were driving through the intersection of Clayton Road and McCausland Avenue, a leak in the gas tank set the car on fire. Switzer and Murphy jumped out and fought the blaze, but it required the services of the St. Louis Fire Department to extinguish it. No one was hurt, but the paper reported that the car sustained $300 worth of damage.

Fred was the family shanachie, the Celtic keeper of the flame, and preserver of family history. He collected photos and letters, visited gravesites, explored archives, corresponded with Murphys and Switzers throughout his life, and recorded an oral history. He lived to the age of 91.

Bernard and Francis were the youngest and the closest, from their days as altar boys at St. Bridget of Erin's in Kerry Patch to the many years they worked side by side at the factory.

Bernard stood not much over five feet tall and would dare anyone to comment on it. He was feisty and rarely reluctant to express his opinion, and he wasn't one to walk away from a fight. Barely out of school, he moved to South Carolina and worked as a jockey. A multi-horse collision ended his racing career, and he returned to St. Louis. His love for horses lasted throughout his life, and he was a frequent judge at St. Louis horse shows. Bernard was always impeccably dressed. "Like he'd just stepped out of a bandbox," his brothers would say.

Francis, the youngest, was the quiet one. His calm manner was a peaceful respite in a temperamental family. He often wore an expression that suggested the first instant of smile, as if he had just thought of something funny and was deciding if he wanted to share it with you. There was a song he learned in the service, which he was fond of singing for no particular occasion:

K-K-K- Katy, beautiful Katy,
You're the only g-g-g-girl that I adore.
When the m-m-m-moon shines over the cow shed,
I'll be waitin' at the k-k-k-kitchen door.

Francis married a young woman named Marion, who was Protestant. Such a thing had never happened in the family before. However, everyone managed to adjust and get through the following decades, and if Marion harbored any resentment for the hoops she jumped through for family and Church, she kept it well hidden. She was known, though, even in her old age, to murmur during a particularly good meal or some especially cheerful occasion that "certainly the Church would not approve of this."

Francis and Fred lived long enough for me to know them both. Uncle Fred would come up from Atlanta to visit his brother in St. Louis, and I remember how the two of them would hold court, bringing back to life their youth in Kerry Patch, their days in the factory, and memories of their brothers. They seemed to have come from the times and places of a separate world.

The United States declared war on Germany on April 6, 1917. Fred enlisted the following day, though he was pushing the age limit at 30. Joe was too old. By summer, Bernard and Francis had enlisted. The three brothers served together as officers in the same unit of the Army Balloon Corps under Major Albert Lambert, training recruits in the balloon and observation skills they would need "over there."

The lives of both soldiers and civilians changed during the 19 months the United States fought in the Great War. With so many men serving in the military, there were more job opportunities for women. Among the many ads in the "Help Wanted" pages of the daily papers, Switzer's offered jobs to "girls" with "good pay and steady work."

The federal government did not impose rationing during World War I, but it did launch a public relations program to curb the public's appetite for many nonessential items, such as sugar. The company continued to manufacture Yellow Jackets, Buttermels, Chocolate Soldiers, and its other sugar-based candies, but increased its production of licorice products. An interesting characteristic of the licorice plant is that it creates its own natural sweetener, so licorice candy served as a backup in case of rising sugar prices or unanticipated rationing.

Fred Murphy (left) and his brother Francis in 1918 while serving in the Balloon Corps. Photo courtesy of the Murphy Family.

Ads in the "Help Wanted" sections of the newspapers referred applicants more frequently to "Switzer's Licorice Company." Even after the war, in 1919, ads offered work to experienced cigar-banders with pay between 18 and 20 dollars a week. The cigars were made of licorice.

The war ended, and Francis and Bernard returned to the factory, but with a different set of expectations. They had commanded men as officers in the US Army and were not inclined to take orders from either Switzer or The Old Gent. Emboldened by their confidence, the two youngest boys were now willing and eager to test the boundaries of business and family.

In early 1920, Francis and Bernard talked Joe and Fred into banding together to start a company called Joseph Murphy Sons & Company. If their father, now 73 years old, had any involvement in the enterprise, it was limited to some initial financial assistance and whatever advice his sons might have requested. They opened shop in an old building around the corner from the factory and began running ads offering jobs to chocolate and icing dippers. On July 25, 1920, the following article ran in the *Post-Dispatch*:

> *Joseph Murphy Sons & Co., for many years in the candy business, have leased 212 North Second Street, a four-story building which, after repairs and alterations are completed, will be occupied as a factory.*

They gave it their best shot, but they had a lot going against them, including a shortage of capital and a lack of marketing experience. The competition from Switzer's must have been intense. Patents kept them from manufacturing any of the products their father had invented, and family pressure from their mother and uncle was surely relentless.

On top of it all, in 1922, The Old Gent packed his trunk once again and sailed off to the Old Sod for another three-month visit. Ireland had just become a Free State, and he certainly knew that he would not have many more opportunities to visit the land in which he was raised, the country he defended, and the home he fled.

Joseph Murphy Sons & Company barely got off the ground before the following announcement appeared in the *Post-Dispatch* on April 22, 1923:

> *Modern, fully-equipped steam plant, in St. Louis for the manufacturing of practically a full line of candies, caramels, fudges, creams, bulk good, bar goods, chocolates, gum work and hard*

candies. This plant is equipped for quality production and will be sold only as unit. To interested parties this is a rare opportunity, and one that will pay you to investigate.

It's easy to imagine that the last nail in the company's coffin might have been an offer from Fred Switzer Sr. to his nephews to return to their old jobs with no hard feelings. In any case, that's what happened. It would have been a victory of sorts for all parties. Joe and Fred Murphy went back out on their own. Their temperaments were too much like their father's. But by 1924, Bernard and Francis returned to 612 N. Main St., rejoining the production department of Switzer's Yellow Jacket Company. It was not the first time that practicality and compromise had soothed over hot tempers and fragile egos to reunite this family of candy makers.

One of their first challenges was the discovery of a side business being run within the factory by a handful of the company's employees. Prohibition had created new markets and a fresh entrepreneurial spirit in America, and some members of the Switzer sanitation and maintenance departments had built a still in the basement and were spending their nights fermenting and bottling the raw materials that had been intended for candy. As the story has been passed on through the decades, it seems that

View of the factory with "Home of Buttermels" painted on the wall, ca. 1920. Photo courtesy of the Murphy Family.

upon being discovered, management agreed to look the other way as long as they made enough only for personal consumption and were not caught by the law. The Switzers and the Murphys apparently had more respect for personal initiative than they did for temperance.

As with any business it had its good days and its bad. February 17, 1928, was certainly one day to remember, when defective wiring on the third floor caused a fire that spread to the fourth floor and caused over $40,000 worth of damage to candy-making machinery and raw materials. The *Globe-Democrat* reported, "Scores of persons gathered on the Eads Bridge . . . to watch firemen pour eight streams of water into the burning structure."

Fortunately, the only person in the building was the night watchman, who escaped uninjured. The plant's sprinkler system helped contain the blaze. Eventually the company recouped its losses.

The 1920s were good years for the candy business. It was a decade of prosperity for many Americans, who had more disposable income than ever. Advertising and product branding developed new levels of sophistication, contributing to an evolving culture of mass consumerism. None of it was lost on Fred Switzer, with his keen marketing instincts, and the company continued to grow in national sales of its candies.

Francis and Bernard had reached a workable peace with their uncle and settled into domestic life. Francis bought the house next door to his parents on Lockwood Avenue, while Bernard, now married, moved into a house just two blocks away. Frederick Switzer had assumed a position of respect in the world of St. Louis business. In 1928, he moved his family into a palatial mansion on a private street in the fashionable suburb of Clayton.

But as the decade of jazz, flivvers, and flappers neared its end, there would be changes—across the nation and within the company.

Promotional display of licorice products, ca. 1925.
Photo courtesy of Switzer's Licorice Archive.

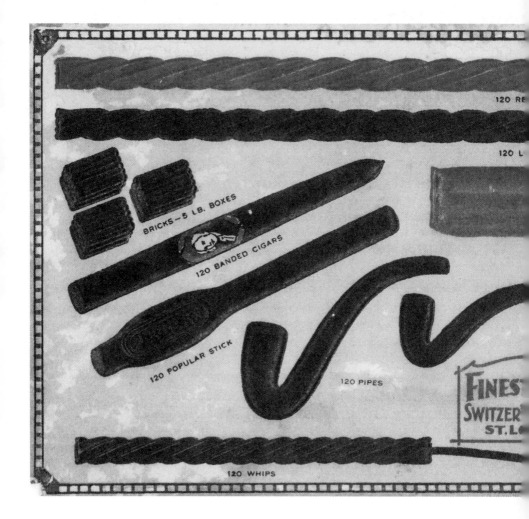

TWIST

TWIST

CHERRY PIE

Switzer's **JUMBO LUNCH BOX**

120 JUMBO LUNCH BOX

ITY
E CO.
D.

S

120 A. B. C. PLUGS

SWITZER'S **QUALITY** BRAND

CIGARETTES ONE CENT

120 CIGARETTES

CHAPTER FIVE

Affordable Luxury

In the early years of the Great Depression, St. Louis had one of the first and largest Hoovervilles in the nation. Named in dubious honor of President Herbert Hoover, the community of more than 5,000 homeless St. Louisans stretched for one mile south of the Municipal (later renamed MacArthur) Bridge. The inhabitants built shelters from orange crates, debris, and wood strewn along the riverbank. Residents lived without electricity and got their water from fire hydrants and rainwater they collected in barrels. It was a community in every sense, with four churches and its own mayor.

Joseph Bernard Murphy didn't live to see much of this decade and the tumultuous changes it brought. The Old Gent died on September 29, 1932, at the age of 85. His life had been a remarkable one, spanning two centuries and two continents.

Hooverville on the St. Louis Riverfront, 1934. Photo courtesy of Missouri History Museum, St. Louis by photographer Isaac Sievers.

The Old Gent, Joseph Bernard Murphy, 1847-1932. Photo courtesy of the Murphy Family.

He had been a nineteenth century revolutionary and a twentieth century capitalist. But he had always been a romantic, believing that it was possible to fight the world's greatest empire with sticks and rocks and that the future could be built upon a foundation of chocolate and caramel.

The world Joseph Murphy left behind was in the midst of its descent into the depths of the Depression. In St. Louis, unemployment was 10 percent in 1930 and would reach 35 percent in 1933. Local government, churches, and nonprofits sponsored soup kitchens and bread lines. Government-sponsored contruction projects, including a new civic auditorium, soldiers' memorial, and federal courthouse, put thousands to work. Unfortunately, the widespread suffering would not come to an end until the start of World War II.

The Depression hit manufacturing in St. Louis harder than in most cities its size. In spite of the revitalization of the brewing industry when Prohibition was repealed in 1933, the city's production of shoes and clothing, steel and iron, chemicals, and food processing was cut in half by the mid-1930s.

St. Louis Riverfront and Downtown on the eve of the Great Depression. Photo courtesy of Missouri History Museum, St. Louis.

One of the few industries spared in St. Louis and across the nation was the candy business. While other manufacturers stalled or went out of business, the demand for candy actually grew. Nationally, new brands, such as Snickers, Tootsie Pops, Payday, Three Musketeers, Red Hots, and Mars Bars, were all invented during the Depression. The history of candy has shown it to be consistently depression-proof. People reward themselves with it during good times and enjoy it as an affordable luxury when life is hard. Switzer's candy rode the rising tide.

The candy shop was a familiar destination in city neighborhoods of the day. A 1947 editorial in the *St. Louis Star and Times* looked back nostalgically on how it felt to be a child in the Depression, staring at a penny candy display while trying to make a decision:

> *Clutching the coppers in hand, one stood before the case breathlessly, more or less mindful of the admonition not to touch the glass and smear it, and one pondered: Ju-jus, neatly wrapped Mary Janes, little orange candy peanuts and bananas, strips of paper with candy polka dots, licorice whips, tiny bottles of wax that had the barest sip of a very sweet liquid in them, giant jawbreakers . . . silver wrapped chocolate drops, caramels, candy cigarettes, Buttermels . . . days of decision, those.*

Candy was a product like no other, providing exotic sensations of sweet, sour, chewy, and tangy that a child would never forget.

As candy sales boomed, the Great Depression brought changes to factories across the country, including Switzer's. Relations between labor and owners were at a low point. In the midst of massive unemployment, many companies felt little pressure to address calls for improving working conditions. A growing number of workers came to see the labor moment as the best path to improving their lives.

The Congress of Industrial Organizations (CIO) began in 1935 as a federation of labor unions. Its founding followed the

National Labor Relations Board's approval earlier that year of labor's right to bargain collectively and operate closed shops. The CIO, which organized craft unions, was particularly aggressive in its organizing tactics, and a wave of strikes swept the county in the mid- and late 1930s.

In October 1937, the United Candy Workers, a CIO affiliate, organized 125 workers at the Switzer Yellow Jacket Company and won recognition as the bargaining agent for its workers. The union negotiated a contract that reduced employees' work week from 45 hours to 40 and granted them a 10 percent wage increase, time and a half for overtime, and a yearly week's vacation with pay.

No industry was better at putting on its happy face than the candy business. The St. Louis Candy Sales Association held a three-day Candy Exposition at the Hotel Jefferson in downtown St. Louis in October 1938. More than 60 national firms set up exhibits at the show. Special events included selection of "The Sweetest in St. Louis Candyland," a competition among women employees of local candy factories, judged by fashion and beauty editors. Along with music and stage entertainment, participants enjoyed kiss-throwing, bubble-gum blowing, and taffy-pulling contests. If that wasn't enough excitement, the city was treated to a candy parade through downtown St. Louis.

Switzer's built candy promotions around just about anything the public was interested in. By the late 1930s, Europe was preparing for war, and though it still seemed a remote possibility that the United States would get involved, interest was growing in all things military. In 1938, Switzer's created a collectors' set of 100 Army Air Corps insignia cards and included them in penny packs of Switzer's Licorice Cigarettes. Youngsters who cut out and sent in 15 cards and 15 cents would receive a full set in four colors.

Switzer realized that the medium of radio offered him the opportunity to deliver his message to even larger audiences. By the end of the decade, the Switzer Candy Company was sponsoring radio station KWK's new quiz show "Fun with Mister Twister," broadcast live from the stage of the Fox Theatre. The company also formed a girls' softball team, appropriately named the Yellow Jackets.

Collect the whole set. An Army Air Corps Insignia card included in Licorice Cigarette Packs, 1938. Photo courtesy of Switzer's Licorice Archive.

The 1930s also saw the American public develop a fascination with gangsters and crime. Movies, magazines, dime novels, and newspaper articles about bad guys were certain to sell. It's worth noting that the Switzer Candy Company had its own brush with the armed and desperate.

The April 14, 1934, edition of the *Globe-Democrat* reported the following incident in a story headlined "Robbers Lose Loot in Hasty Escape":

> *Two bandits, in their haste to flee the scene of their holdup, dropped their loot, which consisted of their victim's pay envelope, with the money, $36, intact. The pair entered the Switzer Candy Company on North Main Street, presented pistols and compelled the night watchman, Joseph R. Smith to descend to the basement, where they bound his hands with rope and tied him to a vertical iron pipe.*

The bandits found Smith's pay envelope in his locker and ran out the back door. Meanwhile, Smith worked himself loose, rushed to the telephone, and found the envelope with his money on the floor. And we learn again that crime does not pay.

During these years a new generation of Switzers joined the company. Fred and Bess' eight children were growing up. His daughters weren't expected to pursue careers, but in 1929, Fred named all five of his sons as legal partners in the company. Their sisters were compensated in equal measure. At the same time, he was clear on the point that just because he owned a factory, his children were not automatically entitled to employment there. As it happened, all of the boys did work at the plant at one time or another, but only two, John and Joe, took on the role of the next generation of Switzer candy men.

John Switzer. Photo courtesy of Tom Switzer.

John, born in 1907, was handsome, dapper, and serious by nature. He spoke when necessary, worked diligently, and took a special interest in the production processes and marketing campaigns of the company. He would eventually assume his father's position as president of the company.

Joe was three years younger and a natural salesman. A talented amateur golfer, he turned his love for the game into a vehicle for promoting the company across the country. From the early

Joseph Switzer. Photo courtesy of Michael Switzer.

1930s to well into the '60s, Joe was a regular fixture in the local sports pages, competing at swanky country clubs, winning titles, and playing exhibition games around the country with sports greats like Ben Hogan. His father encouraged him, and Joe successfully built a network of business and celebrity contacts in St. Louis and across the country.

"My brother and I are watching the Bob Hope Desert Classic one afternoon," recalled his son, Michael. "And all of a sudden we see Dad on the screen hitting the ball up to the green. And Bob Hope is the color man. In those days he actually sat in the booth. And Bob

Hope says, 'There's Joe! Candyman Joe Switzer!' And when dad came home, he brushed it off like it was no big deal. He saw it as his role and what he was supposed to do."

Fred Switzer Jr. was the oldest of the Switzer offspring, and though he never occupied an office at the factory, he played an important role as the respected voice of good sense and wisdom among his siblings. He had earned a law degree from Harvard, a noteworthy achievement for a first generation American Catholic in the 1920s. Among his many accomplishments, Fred Jr. served as the driving force in consolidating the villages of Ladue, Deer Creek, and McKnight into the city of Ladue in 1936. Fred would provide legal assistance to his brothers on an ongoing basis and serve as chairman of the company's board in the 1950s and '60s.

Fred Switzer Jr. Photo courtesy of Tom Switzer.

Fred Jr.'s daughter, Harriet Switzer, remembered her uncles as undemonstrative in their feelings for each other. "The relationship between Fred, Joe, and John tended to be more formal. That's the way it was in our family. The brothers respected one another and dealt with one another in business, but they weren't buddies."

Their parents did their best to protect them from the common side effects of a privileged upbringing, instilling in them a sense of social responsibility and devotion to the Church. Fred Sr., who was not known to have strong religious sentiments, left his children's religious upbringing to Bess, a devoted Catholic. Apparently, it worked. The next generation of Switzers earned a reputation for philanthropy, particularly in matters concerning the Church.

In the mid-1950s, Fred Jr. led a group of Catholic laymen to raise money to buy land for the founding of Saint Louis Priory School in Creve Coeur. At the time, the Church did not encourage young Catholics to attend non-Catholic colleges and universities. Having attended Harvard, Fred Jr. had seen a larger world. Priory was created as a small Catholic boys' high school taught by English Benedictine monks, preparing them for any college they wished to attend. And when St. Anselm, the parish church on the school grounds, was completed, its five bells were donated by the five

A relaxed Fred Switzer Sr. Photo courtesy of Tom Switzer.

brothers. The Switzer boys were well aware that they grew up with advantages, and they knew how far their father had come to provide them.

In spite of his business success, the old man had few pretensions himself. It's true that he was a member of the Missouri Athletic Club, where the elite of St. Louis business hobnobbed. The society columns took regular notice of family weddings and vacations. Bess was president of the Catholic Women's League, as well as the Auxiliary of the Convent of Good Shepherd, and her garden and card parties were always news. But Fred Switzer's greatest pleasures were smoking cigars and listening to Cardinals' baseball on the radio. He was also an accomplished pool player, a skill he acquired growing up in Kerry Patch. To his wife's unending frustration, he preferred to wear his suits until they were threadbare.

"You could say he was scruffy," recalled his granddaughter Harriet. "He never dressed like a wealthy man, never bought new suits, and would not let Grandma touch his clothes.

"He had a chauffeur, Ernie Keys, who drove him for decades. Grandpa never learned to drive. He would get into the back seat of his car at the end of the day to go home, and he'd take off his shoes and stick his feet out the window to air."

Harriet tells the story of how Ernie failed to show up at the factory one day to drive him home, so he decided to hitchhike. The fellow who picked him up followed his directions, driving from downtown into the suburbs. When they finally pulled in front of his Clayton mansion and Fred started to get out, the man tried to stop his down-on-his-luck passenger, until Fred convinced him they were indeed at the right address.

He remained a man of strong opinions throughout his life. His grandson, Fred III, tells a story about one Sunday when he and Bess attended Mass at Our Lady of Lourdes. Apparently unhappy with the priest's homily, he stood up and bellowed, "I don't have to sit here and listen to this," and walked out the door. Bess indeed had her work cut out for her.

By the mid-1930s, the candy company was still a family business, but the dynamics had changed. Fred Sr. was still the undisputed leader of the factory, but he was gradually handing over responsibilities to the next generation. The Murphy and Switzer cousins handled the day-to-day operation of the plant, but the newly arrived Switzer boys had the distinct advantage of being the presumed heirs apparent. For Bernard and Francis, it must have chafed. They had worked at the plant before the war and the Switzer boys were half a generation younger. There was also an unspoken but palpable class distinction. The Murphys had grown up in Kerry Patch; the Switzers, in Kirkwood and Clayton. Fred Switzer's grandson Tom remembered that when he was a child, his mother, a daughter of the Bardenheier wine dynasty, was not amused if anyone made reference to the Switzers' Irish

Left: *Original Murphy and Switzer factory at 11 Main shortly before demolition, late 1930s. Photo courtesy of the Library of Congress.* Right: *Riverfront demolition in progress at Second and Market Streets, 1940. Photo courtesy of Missouri History Museum, St. Louis by photographer Richard Moore.*

background. "Oh, yes," she would say with a touch of disdain, "The Irish," drawing the word into at least three syllables.

The Murphys knew that they and their cousins were bonded by family ties and by their work at the factory, but it was clear they lived in two distinct worlds that did not overlap. Family gatherings became increasingly limited to an occasional wedding or funeral. Nevertheless, for Bernard and Francis, the factory was the center of their world. They felt that the candy company belonged to them as much as it did the Switzers, in a way that transcended legal ownership. It was a sense of possession earned by labor and love.

Throughout the 1930s, an idea was taking shape that would change the face of the city more than any single event since the Great Fire of 1849. A local plan to create a riverfront memorial to Thomas Jefferson and the Louisiana Purchase won approval from the Roosevelt Administration as a means of creating jobs. It took most of the decade to work its way through bureaucratic channels, but on October 9, 1939, Mayor Bernard Dickmann took a crowbar to an old warehouse and knocked out the first brick in what would be a massive demolition of buildings along the riverfront.

The idea caught on quickly as a much-needed economic jump start. The city, along with the entire nation, was still reeling from a Depression with no end in sight. The local real estate industry saw the deteriorating district as a damper on property values west of Third Street. Others saw an unprecedented opportunity to create jobs, and the thought of preserving blocks of narrow streets lined with old factories and warehouses never gained much steam until decades after the deed was done.

There was some opposition to tearing down the last remnant of St. Louis's great manufacturing days. A group of young businessmen organized an effort to place plaques on historic buildings, but there was no stopping the inevitable demolition. Within three years, wrecking crews tore down 40 blocks across 90 acres. The wrecking ball took down almost 500 buildings from Wharf Street to Third Street, and Poplar Street to the Eads Bridge. The Old Cathedral and the Old Courthouse remained standing. Gone was the Murphy and Switzer Candy Company at 11 N. Main St. and Switzer's Yellow Jacket building at 22 N. Main. Bulldozers pushed cast iron facades and nineteenth century architectural details into basements and flattened the ground.

Remnants of St. Louis's manufacturing district, 1941. Photo courtesy of Missouri History Museum, St. Louis, P. R. Papin Aerial Surveys.

For the next 20 years, it would remain a giant patch of rubble. Guarding the wasteland like a watchtower was the candy factory, its giant painted sign proclaiming it to be the home of Switzer's.

Postcard, ca. 1939, highlighting Depression-Era projects, including Civic Center, Federal Building, Civil Courts, and Municipal (Kiel) Auditorium. Photo courtesy of Missouri History Museum, St. Louis.

AIRVIEW ST. LOUIS

CHAPTER SIX

Switzer's Licorice

By 1940, it was apparent to all but the most isolationist of Americans that it was only a matter of time before the United States would enter into what was shaping up to be a second world war. Germany had taken Poland, France, and the Low Countries. England was doing its best to keep Hitler on his side of the English Channel. In St. Louis, the Curtiss-Wright Aircraft Company was starting to fill government orders for planes. An ammunition plant was under construction on the North Side, and a complex in nearby Weldon Spring was producing explosives.

Switzer's Yellow Jacket Company had come through one war, but there had been no rationing during World War I. If access to sugar and butter were limited, the company would have serious problems producing its current line of candies. Rather than wait for rationing and react, the company undertook a major conversion to exclusively produce licorice products.

Licorice had long been an important division of the company. Its penny candy licorice items had sold well since they were first introduced almost 30 years earlier. The Old-Fashioned Licorice Bar, introduced in 1932, was successfully competing in the newly emerging candy bar market. Now Switzer's was replacing all of the old brands. And just in time. Predictions of rationing were on target. Sugar was the first consumer commodity to be rationed in the spring of 1942. The following year, butter and dairy products were on the list. However, the main ingredients of licorice candy were corn syrup, flour, and molasses, and those were readily available.

Advertisements in magazines were still offering a pound of "Sweeter than Honey" Yellow Jackets for 19 cents a pound at Walgreens in 1939. But by the summer of 1940, the company was promoting a new product, the Switzer's Old-Fashioned Licorice Twist. Soon to follow the black licorice twists were bites, bars, and sticks. A 1943 daily stock inventory sheet included such licorice products as Long Jumbos, Licorice Cigarettes and Cigars, Plugs, Black Whips, Pipes, and something called the Licorice Block.

Oh Boy! It's Good!

SWITZER'S
Old-Fashioned
LICORICE TWIST
"Best By Taste"

In the Original
5¢
PACKAGE

Early advertisement promoting Switzer's shift to all-licorice production, 1940. Photo courtesy of Switzer's Licorice Archive.

Licorice's recorded history goes back to the Pharaohs, Julius Caesar, and Alexander the Great, who were all said to enjoy drinking a licorice-based concoction for their health. By the seventeenth century, licorice had found its way to England, where monks at the monastery in Pontefract discovered their sandy soil was perfect for cultivating the plant. They created a small industry, manufacturing a medicinal licorice cake, which they eventually exported to North America.

The licorice plant, or *Glycyrrhiza glabra*, as some like to call it, is a leafy cousin of the pea and grows to a height of about three feet. Primarily found in Syria, Turkey, Iraq, and parts of Southern Europe, its root can be processed into a sweet paste, which emits the strong anise-like flavor and aroma that dominated the St. Louis Riverfront for so many years. Compounds in the licorice make it up to 50 times sweeter than sugar. Beyond its role as a candy ingredient, licorice extract also adds flavor and reduces harshness in tobacco products.

The licorice root has long been the darling of medical studies, hailed with varying degrees of credibility as a source of relief from ulcers, fungal infections, canker sores, chronic bronchitis, menstrual cramps, and hot flashes. Fred Switzer saw it as a source of relief from sugar rationing, and by the time the United States had entered World War II, he had renamed his entire operation Switzer's

Licorice Company. What had been a small division of the operation had become the heart and the future of the company.

Retooling a nineteenth-century factory that was producing a variety of chocolate and caramel candies into an efficient, twentieth-century plant creating a completely different product was a major undertaking. The production department dismantled much of the old equipment and stored it in a warehouse down the street. New machines were utilized, but the challenges were immense. The factory was five stories high, and the only way to get from one floor to another was by using an antiquated elevator or the stairwells. There was no warehouse and only limited storage space. To make it even trickier, the licorice required a process more like baking bread than making traditional penny candies.

To enter the front door of the Switzer Licorice Company was to pass into another world of continuous human and mechanical

View of the Switzer factory and Eads Bridge, 1948. Photo courtesy of Missouri History Museum, St. Louis by photographer Dick Lemen.

motion, dominating the senses with the thick smell of licorice and a cacophony of industrial noises. The floors were giant, brightly lit spaces filled with machinery and conveyor tracks moving licorice to various stages of completion, from one floor to another—some at waist level, others passing overhead on belts and rollers.

In the basement, or "the kitchen" as it was called, men dumped 100-pound bags of flour and water into a giant mixer, creating a slurry that they pumped through pipes into a row of giant kettles. Then syrup, corn starch, salt, licorice extract, anise oil, and other ingredients flowed from pipes into the kettles. The concoction cooked for at least two hours before being discharged into 150-pound tubs where it sat for at least two days until it jelled.

Conveyers pulled the tubs from the basement to the upper floors, where workers plopped the heavy slabs onto rollers that fed them through extruders, "slicing them into sizes and shapes appropriate for bars, bites, or twists.

Teams of women placed the newly cut licorice pieces on trays, stacked them on racks, and wheeled them into drying rooms. Sometimes the conveyors ran too fast for the women to keep up, spilling the licorice onto the floor.

From the drying rooms, the racks of licorice moved to packaging tables, where other teams wrapped them by hand, put them in boxes, and placed them on conveyors that would roll them down to the first floor and out the door. Drivers, waiting at the curb in front of the factory, pulled the boxes from the conveyors and loaded them onto their trucks. It was a process driven by machines, muscle, fire, and gravity.

The work could be tiring, boring, and sometimes dangerous, but a camaraderie developed among the workers, which many of them recalled fondly in later years. In the early 1990s, one employee, Juanita Hejmej, reflected on her years working on the line with the other women. She remembered that during the war years a steady flow of troop trains ran along the elevated tracks by the river. Servicemen trying to get to Union Station would disembark at a small depot behind the factory and walk to the Eads Bridge where they could make their transfers. Juanita remembered that even though it was not allowed, she and her co-workers would wave to the boys from the large open windows. In later years she would wonder how many survived the war. "Sometimes I think it would be wonderful to have a reunion with these girls," she said. "It's all long gone, but never forgotten."

Beyond the changes the war years brought to the factory, they also brought losses to both the Murphy and the Switzer sides of the family. The indomitable Margaret Catherine Switzer lived another 12 years after the death of her husband, reigning from her Webster Groves home as the Murphy family matriarch. She died on December 28, 1944, at the age of 80. She presented herself as a stern and somewhat intimidating figure in her later years. Some younger family members found her particularly frightening, but they would not have known about the poverty of Kerry Patch, the loss of her daughter Kate, or the hardship of raising four boys while married to a man born to roam. Throughout her long life, she never lost her fierce loyalty to her Switzer family, her loving devotion to her Murphy sons, or her determination to overcome whatever stood in her way to protect those she loved.

Maybe it was fortunate that she died when she did. Had she lived a few years longer, she would have suffered the loss of two of her sons. Her oldest, Joe Jr., lived his life with a mix of easy charm and spotty luck. He remarried after the death of his first wife, Josephine, but an uneven temper and poor health would make his life more difficult than it needed to be. While in his 50s, his eyesight began to fail. He died on October 6, 1945. The headline in the *Post-Dispatch* read: "Blind Man Killed in Fall from Hospital." The coroner reported the cause of his death as "fracture of the skull . . . when he jumped from a third-floor room of Deaconess Hospital." The Church showed discretion and proclaimed it an accident, and he was buried beside his mother and father in consecrated ground in the Murphy-Switzer plot in Calvary Cemetery.

Bernard, the feisty son, who worked so closely and so long with his brother Francis at Switzer's, died of a heart attack on the factory floor on April 22, 1948.

When the war ended, Switzer's continued with its all-licorice product line. Licorice had sold well during the war, it could be produced efficiently in a variety of shapes and sizes, and re-converting the factory would have been a massive and expensive enterprise.

Working conditions had improved considerably since the early days of the candy company, when workers had no bargaining rights and no representation. The Candy Workers Union had done its part in giving a voice to the workers, but there was still room for improvement, and more changes would come. The story of Alice Phelps, a Switzer employee who insisted that her voice be heard, became an inspiration to Switzer's workers and a company legend.

Alice was a young woman when she joined the plant at the end of the war. Jobs were scarce, so she was happy to have the work. But Switzer's had a "No Talk Rule," forbidding conversation that was not work-related. And Alice was a talker.

As the weeks passed and her frustration grew, she developed a plan. She chose a specific Monday a few weeks away and whispered to every non-supervisory woman in the factory that this day would be "Talk Monday." At the beginning of their shifts they would begin talking and would not stop until the day was over. Surely, the company would not fire them all.

"Talk Monday" arrived, and after some initial hesitation conversations among the women of Switzer's Licorice were in full swing. After a while, the astonished men followed the example of their female colleagues and joined in. Everyone was still making licorice, but they were talking, and even the anger of stunned supervisors could not stop them.

As the legend goes, Fred Switzer stopped the production lines and, flanked by his managers, gathered the entire workforce to tell them that this rebellion was unacceptable. He was, he said, a good employer and insisted that the company's rules be respected.

But the resistance continued, and in spite of efforts to root out the instigators, no one informed on Alice. As it turned out, chatting employees did not cut into production numbers. "Talk Mondays" became company policy, leading to an eventual easing of all rules regarding reasonable human communication.

Alice, immensely popular among both managers and workers, eventually became the chief steward for Teamsters Local 688, representing the majority of Switzer's employees. In tribute to her, one of the giant kettles in the factory's basement was named "Big Alice."

Frederick Switzer Sr. was 80 years old when the war ended. He had spent most of his life focused on his work, but now he found more pleasure spending time with his family, particularly his many grandchildren. He was known to be as kind at home as he was tough at work. His grandson, Fred III, recalled fondly, "He smoked cigars and he always carried licorice in his breast pocket, and he'd grab me and pick me up and give me a great big hug and a kiss, and I was bathed in that aroma of cigars and licorice."

In the autumn of 1949, he contracted a cold. It wasn't a particularly bad one, and after a couple of days he seemed to be improving. On Sunday morning, October 23, he was drinking

South wall of the factory, 1950. Photo courtesy of Switzer's Licorice Archive.

coffee and reading the newspaper while his wife Bess and son Joe attended seven o'clock Mass at Our Lady of Lourdes. Thirty minutes later, he suffered a pulmonary embolism and died instantly. He was 84 years old.

Frederick Michael Switzer's body was placed near the fireplace at his Clayton home for his wake, with more than 500 mourners paying their respects. Archbishop Joseph Ritter called Bess to offer his condolences. Fred left more than 20 grandchildren, and in the midst of the funeral arrangements, his son, Fred Jr., wrote a letter to his son Fred III. It was a tribute to the Switzer patriarch:

> He was very proud of the name of Switzer and of what he had succeeded in making it stand for. While he had the means to indulge in practically any luxury or enjoyment that he chose, he refrained from all but the simplest pleasures and possessions. He built for his family, and his joy was in their welfare.

In business he had always played to win, driven by his passion and his wits to build a company and outmaneuver his competitors. He had known poverty and was determined that his family never would. And though his wife and children were probably more concerned with the state of his soul than he, Fred Jr. wrote that his father had taken time to reflect upon his long life just a day before his death:

> Happily, we can all rest assured that he has accomplished God's will. He liked to review his life and spoke to me about it Saturday afternoon. He concluded very seriously that he had nothing to worry about and with that I can well agree.

The operation of the company continued much as it had for years. John was the boss and his brother Joe continued to travel across the country, playing golf and drumming up clients. Their cousin, Francis Murphy, was plant manager, running the daily operation of making licorice. However, the post-war era brought a sense that the world would not be the same. Designs of automobiles and architecture were reflecting changes in popular taste. Big bands were making room for new genres of popular music, including the morally dubious rock 'n' roll. A new

Frederick Michael Switzer, 1865–1949. Photo courtesy of Tom Switzer.

highway system was taking families out of the city and turning cornfields into subdivisions.

A new Switzer's letterhead reflected the spirit of post-war pizzazz. A bright, streamlined version of the old factory rose above a grid of parks, fountains, and modernist sculptures along the river. As fanciful as this view of the future might have been, it communicated the optimism of the day. Not wanting to be left behind, Switzer's began making some changes to modernize the plant and bring its products more in line with these modern times.

One of the first changes was in the overall look of the packaging and displays. Spending more money than the company had ever invested in a marketing plan, the Switzers hired a firm to create a new image. In 1950, Switzer's Old-Fashioned Licorice presented itself with a not so-old-fashioned look. Newspaper ads and display boxes took on a new eye-catching contrast of bright yellow against black. The company created a dime package of licorice. Cartoon twins, Hy'Enjoyment and Lo'Calorie, declared in newspaper and magazine ads that they were "best together in delicious Switzer's Licorice" as they biked, swam, skated, golfed,

SWITZER'S LICORICE COMPANY

612 NORTH FIRST STREET·
JEFFERSON MEMORIAL PLAZA
SAINT LOUIS, (2) MISSOURI

Modernizing the brand. 1947 letterhead. Photo courtesy of Switzer's Licorice Archive.

and performed acrobatics in newspaper and magazine ads. Gone forever were the days of "Oh, Boy, It's Good!"

In an effort to cut production costs, Switzer's hired a project engineer by the name of Clarence Block to automate certain elements of the candy-making process. Block had already streamlined Sara Lee's assembly line and invented a system that would evenly space pecans in its coffee cake. A born tinkerer, he was also credited with the creation of Roy Rogers action figures for Post Cereals and the double-sided dog dish, offering pups both food and water in one convenient device.

There were signs that the public wanted a red candy, but Switzer's was at first reluctant to develop it, believing that without molasses, licorice extract, and anise oil, it wouldn't be genuine licorice. But the company bowed to popular demand in 1959 and began

Trade ad with the newly created "Switzer Twins", 1953. Photo courtesy of Switzer's Licorice Archive.

producing Switzer's Cherry Red. In years to come, its sales would outstrip by far the traditional black licorice.

The Switzer brothers considered the possibility of expanding their operation to include a new factory in the East. Pennsylvania and New York had long been particularly large markets for their licorice. In 1955, articles appeared in Pennsylvania newspapers, reporting that the Switzer Licorice Company was developing a plan to build a plant near the small town of Stroudsburg, Pennsylvania. The Pocono Mountain Chamber of Commerce went as far as proposing to finance a $300,000 structure, sell stock to local residents, and conduct a study on the labor environment there. The understanding was

Ad for retailers with Switzer's new look, mid 1950s. Photo courtesy of Switzer's Licorice Archive.

that Switzer's might employ as many as 150 people. Nothing came of the plan, but it was clear that the company was open to broadening its national presence and, with a factory in Pennsylvania, planting itself directly in the Hershey Company's front yard.

It's worth noting that the Pocono plan included a study on the labor force. Since the end of the war, important changes had occurred in Switzer's relationship with organized labor. Union efforts during the Great Depression had already given some voice to Switzer's workers and earned them the basic rights that labor was demanding across the country. But there would be more

changes, bringing an even bigger
shift in the power balance between
management and workers.

There is a pervasive myth that
during World War II, American labor
and management put their differences
aside for the sake of victory over the Axis.
In fact, the opposite was true. Both the
CIO and its rival American Federation of
Labor (AFL) made a no-strike pledge for the
duration, but union members across
the country staged thousands of wildcat
strikes and work stoppages to gain
concessions from employers reluctant
to risk war contracts. Immediately after the war, so many strikes
occurred that in 1947 a nervous Congress passed the Taft-Hartley
Act, severely restricting labor's right to organize.

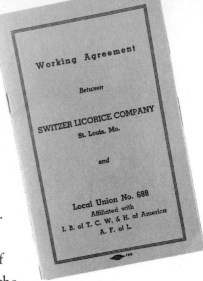

Teamsters Local 688 Handbook for
Switzer's employees, 1950. Photo
courtesy of Thomas H. Eliot Personal
Papers, Washington University Libraries.

The same forces were at play in St. Louis and at Switzer's. But
the labor scene in St. Louis was particularly interesting due to the
large role played by a man named Harold Gibbons. Gibbons was
tall and good-looking, a tough guy and a visionary, and a practical
man who played the game when necessary but was not afraid to
buck even his own membership to do what he believed best for
the community. He joined the labor movement in the late 1930s,
organizing and leading strikes for the CIO. In 1941, the union
sent him to St. Louis to tame a rebellious local of warehouse
workers. Instead, they won him over, and by the late 1940s he
shed his allegiance to the more radical CIO and was leading
warehouse workers into a new union, Teamsters Local 688, a
St. Louis AFL affiliate.

Local 688 was on its way to becoming St. Louis's most powerful
union. On September 4, 1950, it negotiated a contract with

Switzer's Licorice, representing 115 of its 180 employees, most of whom were women. The workforce had come a long way since its "Pretty Gum Wrappers Union" in 1900. By 1952, the local had enough clout to call in Thomas H. Eliot, a prominent national political figure and the current chair of Washington University's political science department, to arbitrate a dispute. Production Manager Francis Murphy wanted to fire two employees for fighting on the factory floor. Eliot found in favor of the workers.

In 1953, with the help of Teamsters Vice President Jimmy Hoffa, Harold Gibbons thwarted an attempt by East Side crime boss Frank "Buster" Wortman to control the local. In 1955, the CIO rejoined the AFL after a 17-year separation, and Gibbons rose to the top positions of labor leadership in the city. That year, Teamsters Local 688 represented 60 percent of the workers at 130 St. Louis firms, where the average hourly wage was $1.70 and rising.

Unlike many union leaders of the time, Gibbons was concerned with social issues that transcended the typical union focus on working conditions and wages. He recruited African American political activist and union organizer Ernest Calloway as his assistant. Together they fought for integration of public facilities and the public schools, years before the landmark *Brown vs. Topeka* Supreme Court ruling.

Gibbons threw the support of the Teamsters behind the creation of the Bi-State Development Agency, Community College District, and Metropolitan Sewer District. He set up community service centers where union members would help neighborhoods deal with daily issues like garbage pickup, the placement of bus stops, and removal of dead trees. It was a grassroots vision of a union operating at every level of the community for better living conditions.

But from the perspective of management at a small factory like Switzer's, the power of Local 688 was a challenge. Policy decisions were no longer made unilaterally or even negotiated on an even level. The union held the chips, and there were no decisions too small to ignore the union's position. The years ahead would be generally peaceful and free of work stoppages, but the possibility of a strike was always there and every bit as effective as the real thing.

A new decade arrived, and the factory lost another member of its second generation of candy men. Francis Murphy, the youngest son of The Old Gent, had worked at the factory since its earliest days. He'd helped orchestrate the conversion from chocolate and caramel candies to licorice. He was the last at the plant to remember the company's origins in Kerry Patch or understand how the operation had been shaped over time by the personalities of his strong-willed father and uncle. He worked as plant manager until a year before his death in 1960. Upon Francis' death, there was still one more generation to whom the mantle would be passed.

Francis Murphy Jr. was my father. He went by Frank. He was charming and smart, and I can't imagine him without a cigarette dangling from the corner of his mouth. He smelled like licorice and Lucky Strikes. The man could swear too, stringing together paragraphs of epithets with the rhythm and colors of a poem. He joined the Navy when he was 18 and was ready to ship out to Japan when Truman dropped the bomb and saved him the trip.

After the War, he moved to New York for a while and tried to write a novel. Then he worked as an announcer at a couple of St. Louis radio stations. He returned to civilian life determined never to let anyone tell him what to do. That included Holy Mother Church. No force on earth could get him to Mass, but he had that small crucifix his grandfather brought to America on his dresser as long as I can remember, and sometimes when I was a kid I'd catch him praying in secret when we were together in the car. I knew what he was doing, because he would pretend to

Frank Murphy. Photo courtesy of the Murphy Family.

scratch his chest when he was really making the sign of the cross.

Frank was more comfortable with humanity as a concept than with individual people. Buying him Father's Day cards was always tough, because most of them had fishing poles or baseball mitts on the cover, and he wasn't a fishing pole-baseball mitt kind of guy. He wasn't family-man material, but by 1949 he had a family anyway and needed a real job, so he went down to Switzer's and worked alongside his father. It wasn't the life he dreamed of, but it was the one he got. And he was good at it. When his father died, he assumed the position of production superintendent. He probably thought he'd work there the rest of his life. I remember he kept a copy of *Walden* on his desk.

EAT and ENJOY

LOW CALORIE CANDY

Switzer's

Low Calorie

10¢
Old Fashioned
LICORICE
SWITZER'S LICORICE COMPANY
BUY IT HERE!
10¢
Candy

CHAPTER SEVEN

Under New Management

Over a period of 200 years, the stretch of land south of the Switzer factory had changed from a forest atop a bluff to a fur trading post, then a village, a manufacturing district, and finally a wasteland. The 1960s would see its transformation into a national park.

The construction of Eero Saarinen's masterpiece, a 630-foot stainless steel arch, brought a kind of international attention to which the city was unaccustomed. The Gateway Arch would be the tallest manmade monument in the Western Hemisphere. Newspapers and television stations shot thousands of photographs and newsreels of its construction from the groundbreaking on February 12, 1963, to its completion on October 28, 1966. Peeking from the background of many was the factory, with "Home of Switzer's Licorice and Cherry Red Candy" emblazoned on its wall. The Arch was a symbol of a new St. Louis, re-branded as the Gateway to the West. And once again, the factory by the bridge had a front row seat to history.

Demolition continued to be the city's tool of choice in dealing with rundown neighborhoods like the old riverfront. By the time the arch was topped off, the city had just finished tearing down 5,600 buildings in a 465-acre swath through the Mill Creek neighborhood. The project displaced about 20,000 residents, mostly African Americans, between Union Station and St. Louis University. Demolition throughout the city was ongoing and sporadic. There was even a short-lived plan to tear down the Central West End and build a mini city of the future in its place.

A concern for historic preservation would come later. At the time, it made sense to sweep away the old and build anew. There was a heady, optimistic mood among St. Louis boosters that the city was at the dawn of a new day. The nation watched the Cardinals beat the Yankees in the 1964 World Series and voters chose the charismatic Alfonso Cervantes as their mayor in 1965. A new downtown stadium opened in May of 1966, and more highways and office towers were on the drawing board.

Switzer's felt it was time for some updating of its own to get into sync with what people were starting to call the "Soaring Sixties." The company hired a New York motivational research firm to study the company and submit a "Creative Memo" with advice on how best to move ahead. The 31-page report, speaking largely in the psycho-babble of its day, reflected upon such things as "the true meaning of licorice" and how it can "meet the challenge of the changing candy climate."

The nature of that challenge, it surmised, was that licorice lived in a new and modern world in which consumers placed more value on achieving pleasure and new experiences. Licorice, however, bore the same baggage of guilt as most candies, linked to self-indulgence, weight gain, and tooth decay. Licorice specifically reminded candy buyers of penny candy and the Great Depression, which the report called the "era of low income." In short, "Licorice had not kept pace and has not produced a modern picture of its product."

Women working on the Switzer licorice line. Photo courtesy of Renyold Ferguson for the St. Louis Post-Dispatch/Polaris.

Whatever was a candy company to do? The motivational research company advised Switzer's to dramatize the personal meanings of candy and introduce it as the new taste adventure. The most practical advice was to introduce some new, flashier packaging and fix its cellophane bags so they didn't immediately fall apart when customers opened them.

The report urged more emphasis on what it called licorice's therapeutic values. "Licorice," it advised, "should be presented as the light, natural, wholesome, nourishing, non-fattening, non-allergic candy." That might be helped by a new company symbol that would introduce a modern touch without losing traditional appeal. It suggested a graphic design derived from the licorice plant.

One of the final warnings concerned the problematic nature of the company's name. Apparently, Switzer didn't roll off the tongue as smoothly as Mars or Hershey. The report noted, "At the present time there is confusion in saying or reading the name. This might be accomplished by the spoken word—on TV or radio, as well as some phonetic written presentation of the name."

It's difficult to imagine how John and Joe Switzer responded. Not so difficult to picture Joseph Murphy and Frederick Switzer pouring over the report in stunned silence.

The *Globe-Democrat* reported in November 1964 that John Switzer announced the company had outgrown its riverfront plant and was considering several other locations, including an industrial park in Crestwood, Missouri. The plan didn't materialize, but it did telegraph a shaky commitment to remaining in its historic place by the river. The company wasn't doing poorly. Annual sales had grown to $6.5 million. Over 200 employees were manufacturing black and red licorice in a variety of shapes and sizes. The company was poised to take the next step, but no one was quite sure what that would be.

Frank Murphy brought his own style to the job of production manager. He had a talent for electronics and machinery, which he applied in various ways to improve the production line. Distrustful of authority, and considerably younger than his Switzer cousins, he preferred the company of the machinists, workers, and union officials to that of other managers. He liked being an outsider, and he saw possibilities in the factory that went beyond making licorice.

Murphy, like a growing number of white St. Louisans in the 1960s, began to see St. Louis's Jim Crow past for the first time. Sit-ins at Woolworth's, a boycott of Jefferson Bank, and even a protest that stopped work at the partially completed Arch sparked a spirit of idealism and social consciousness throughout the region. Civil rights organizations, unions, nonprofits, and churches were reaching out to local businesses to become a part of the solution.

Murphy was the company's point man in a partnership with the old Kerry Patch parish of St. Bridget of Erin. The neighborhood had long ago transitioned from Irish to African American, but otherwise little had changed. St. Bridget's pastor, Fr. John Shockley, created a jobs program to address large-scale unemployment in the neighborhood. Prison records, alcohol and drug addiction, poor luck, and bad decisions by its residents were discouraging local companies from hiring them. During his time as production manager, Murphy provided a steady source of jobs and training at the candy factory. He never said as much, but the collaboration offered him a side entrance to a back pew in the Church he had never quite left.

The primary business of Switzer's Licorice was making candy, and regardless of whatever improvements its management team brought to society or to its own facility, one fact remained: It was making licorice in a 90-year-old, gravity-driven factory with five stories and no warehouse, competing with companies that had modernized years earlier.

Fred Switzer III, like his father Fred Switzer Jr., was an attorney and handled occasional legal work for the company. He believed that a major obstacle to growth was Switzer's contract with the Teamsters, keeping labor costs high and complicating managerial decisions. In the mid-1960s, he advised his uncles to close the St. Louis plant and move the entire operation to a right-to-work state. John and Joe, he argued, could hire a manager to supervise daily production, and they could manage the big picture from St. Louis. His uncles would have no part of the plan. The union had become a kind of partner over the years, even if not quite one of the family.

A more serious problem was that the company had no plan of succession when John and Joe would eventually retire. Their niece, Harriet, remembered family discussions on the issue.

"My father (Fred Jr.) was chairman of the board at the time, and he realized there was no one in the family who was able to succeed John or Joe. None of the cousins seemed able to do that kind of thing. Or were interested. Or [they] were too young. So Dad saw the writing on the wall that there wasn't a Switzer around who was able to carry on the family name."

And then an unexpected solution presented itself. In the mid-1950s, Beatrice Foods, a food processing company headquartered in Chicago, was acquiring companies that made specialty food products. Their growth in the area of confections and snacks began in 1955 when they bought the D.L. Clark Company, maker of the Clark Bar. Beatrice was particularly interested in candies that had already established themselves as popular brands. Over the next decade, Beatrice acquired Jolly Rancher, maker of Stix Bars, and M.J. Holloway, which produced Milk Duds and Slo Pokes. Over time, the Confectionery and Snack Division would include some of the best-known candies and snacks in America.

Beatrice's eye fell upon Switzer's, and its overtures were kindly received. It seemed like a good match. Beatrice, with its vast resources, could pump new life into Switzer's, which had a national reputation but was underperforming, with no clear course for the future. On October 16, 1966, an article in the Business Section of the *Post-Dispatch* announced the sale:

> *Merger of the Switzer Licorice Co. and Beatrice Foods Co., Chicago was announced here Thursday. Fred M. Switzer, Jr. is board chairman of the St. Louis firm, manufacturers of a nationally known line of licorice and candies. He said the company would operate here as a Division of Beatrice with the same management, personnel and products.*

The Switzer family received the equivalent of $6 million in stock. John and Joe Switzer continued in their old positions but reported to Beatrice. Leaving current management in place was the typical procedure in Beatrice acquisitions. The thinking behind this "decentralized management" plan was that by providing the old bosses, who knew best how their companies worked, with fresh resources, capital, and advice, Beatrice's investments would begin paying off from day one. It was a strategy that generally worked. Not so well at Switzer's.

Three and one-half years after Beatrice's purchase, Switzer's was declining in sales and profit, a fact that came to the attention of top management in Chicago. In early 1970, Beatrice offered the position of Switzer's General Manager and Executive Vice President to a 33-year-old executive named Bob Kill. Kill had worked for Beatrice since 1959, but this was to be his first management job, and he was eager to show that he had what it took to turn the situation around. He recalled, "After I was offered the job, William G. Karnes, Beatrice's CEO, stopped by my desk and told me I had to 'pull the St. Louis knife out of his back.' He promised to come to St. Louis and throw a big dinner party for all of the Switzer's employees when our earnings exceeded one million dollars."

Kill arrived in St. Louis in April of 1970, which was the worst possible time. A wildcat strike by rebellious Teamsters had

End of an era. Mayor Alfonso Cervantes (second from left) joins Beatrice and Switzer leadership to complete the sale. October 13, 1966. Photo courtesy of the St. Louis Public Library by photographer Peter Ferman.

idled thousands of trucks across the country, paralyzing freight movements in major cities and resulting in widespread layoffs. Tensions ran high. Armed men were stopping rigs on interstate highways and forcing drivers to abandon their trucks. In St. Louis there was a total truck shutdown by 9,500 Teamsters. Because every box of Switzer's Licorice had to be put on a truck, one of Kill's first acts was to shut the factory down for six weeks.

His next surprise was the lack of any post-acquisition company strategy. "There was nothing," he remembered. "No plans on my desk, no reports, no strategic plan. I needed to improve profitability, lower labor costs, lower production costs, raise prices, or shut it down. I wondered why the hell Beatrice had bought the place."

There was clearly a misunderstanding. The Switzers seemed to have interpreted the hands-off relationship as a green light for business as usual. Beatrice was expecting Switzer's to borrow upon

Beatrice's capital and expertise to make substantial improvements and increase volume. John and Joe had spent years taking the plant as far as it could go. The factory was old, the relationship with the union was well entrenched, and the manufacturing processes had been tweaked to their limits. It wasn't theirs any more, anyway. Beatrice saw it as a profit center that needed to pull its weight within the division. It was offering Switzer's management the freedom to figure out the problems and the resources to get them fixed.

John retired shortly after Kill arrived. Joe left after about a year. Kill particularly liked Joe but wasn't sure the feeling was reciprocal. "I got along well with him, liked him, and respected him" he said. "But I suspect he did not enjoy my aggressive approach to sales and marketing."

It was a classic collision of cultures. The old ways, set in motion by Murphy and Switzer in an earlier century, still prevailed. The sales department was located in an office across the street from the factory, a relic of the old divisions between the founding salesman and the founding candy maker. The company's culture, developed over more than 80 years, dictated that efficiency should always take a back seat to the quality of the finished product. Switzer's was still basically a nineteenth-century family-operated factory in a twentieth-century corporate world.

Kill had inherited a tough situation. It was his first shot on the front lines. The CEO of Beatrice Foods was waiting for results. He wasn't getting a lot of help from St. Louis management. Nothing about this was going to be easy, but what he did have going for him was drive and confidence.

Jim Clark was Beatrice's quality control manager. He remembered his first impression of his boss: "Bob Kill was tall and good looking, lots of dark hair, carefully dressed. If you were going to cast someone in a movie as a young executive, moving up to be vice president, casting Bob Kill would be very believable."

Kill began turning things around. Profits were back on the upswing and production had increased to the point where the plant had maxed out its capacity. In 1972, he opened a second factory, in a more modern industrial space at 1600 N. Broadway, not far from the Landing. It provided many of the amenities that the old

Switzer's Licorice joins the Beatrice family. Photo courtesy of Switzer's Licorice Archive.

factory did not, including a warehouse and the ability to conduct production on a single floor. Beatrice had begun purchasing more modern equipment capable of producing products more quickly and inexpensively, but there would be no real change until the last vestiges of the old methods were eliminated.

Among Kill's top priorities were containing labor costs, but Teamsters Local 688 had been a part of the company's decision-making process for so many years that it was not possible to simply cut jobs or reduce wages. The simplest production processes involving labor had been negotiated and re-negotiated so many times that they were nearly cast in stone, and changes were difficult. A second priority was reducing other production costs, but the company's culture had long protected its hallowed recipes and production processes.

Bob Kill fired Frank Murphy in 1972. "I'm pushing for change, and it isn't happening fast enough," he explained. "I'm sorry that it

Switzer's transitions to a new factory on Broadway after 1972. Photo courtesy of Switzer's Licorice Archive.

had to be done, but it had to be done, and Frank was not surprised, and, I think, he seemed relieved."

Years later, Kill recalled that Murphy was caught in an impossible situation, between the old Switzer way of managing the plant and the aggressive bottom-line expectations that he, Kill, imposed on him. For Murphy, it was a failure on several levels. He'd not only lost his job, but he'd left unfinished the work his family had begun two generations ago and had passed on to him. Working at the plant may have not been his first choice of how to spend his life, but it was too late now to write the novel or work as a broadcaster. He had worked hard to be a Candy Man, but the world had changed around him and made that impossible.

And that is how the era of the family factory came to an end. Switzer's Licorice reached its $1 million profit goal that year. CEO William G. Karnes came to St. Louis and threw a big party for all of the employees. Kill was promoted to executive vice president of Beatrice's Confectionery and Snack Division in 1973. The following years would see him rise from head of the division to corporate vice president. But there was one major bump in the road waiting just around the corner.

figures don't lie...
it's the
LOW CALORIE
Candy

Figures show, sweet delicious SWITZER'S is lower in calories than most other popular candy bars. Get a bar at your favorite candy counter.

SWITZER'S - ST. LOUIS

The Delmar Cream, one of a variety of products
offered by Switzer's Yellow Jacket Company, 1920s.
Photo courtesy of Switzer's Licorice Archive.

Switzer's
5¢
Old Fashioned
LICORICE TWIST
SWITZER'S LICORICE COMPANY
ST. LOUIS, MO.

A jar and box of the Old Fashioned Twists, leading
the way to a wartime all-licorice product line, 1940.
Photo courtesy of Switzer's Licorice Archive.

Letterhead promoting the company's licorice division as "Switzer's Licorice Company", 1930s. Photo courtesy of Switzer's Licorice Archive.

Jumbo Twists, an early licorice product by "Switzer's Licorice Co.", ca. 1915. Photo courtesy of Switzer's Licorice Archive.

Display box for Popular Sticks, a licorice penny candy, ca. 1915. Photo courtesy of Switzer's Licorice Archive.

The kids loved Switzer's Cigars, ca. 1920.
Photo courtesy of Switzer's Licorice Archive.

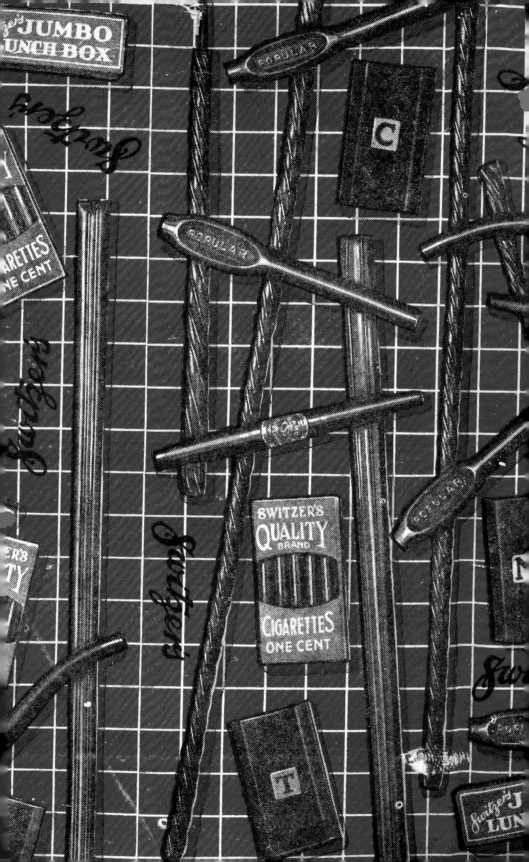

The "New Look" in branding for the 1960s.
Photo courtesy of Switzer's Licorice Archive.

HOME OF

Switzer's
Licorice and
Cherry Red candy

View looking north toward the factory, 1970s.
Photo courtesy of Switzer's Licorice Archive.

Cherry Red bars roll out from the continuous extrusion process, ca. 1980. Photo courtesy of Jim Clark.

Last days of the famous Switzer sign as crews tear down the factory, 2007. Photo courtesy of Switzer's Licorice Archive.

Switzer's Licorice changes hands as a new downtown takes shape, 1967.
Photo courtesy of Missouri History Museum, St. Louis, photographer Ted McCrea.

CHAPTER EIGHT
Fade to Black

Ultimately there was only one way to bring production costs down to a point where Beatrice could earn an acceptable profit, and that was to change the essential process that made the candy. The open-kettle process the company had used for decades required at least three days to go from mixing to cooking to packaging. There was, however, a new method already being used by other companies that could accomplish all that in less than 20 minutes. It was called the "continuous extrusion process," and Beatrice was buying new machinery to try it out at its new plant on Broadway. It would be a major change in the way Switzer's made its licorice, so the transition would have to be brought about carefully. It was critical that the public not detect any change in the product.

Jim Clark was a scientist and a quality control expert. He joined Beatrice in March of 1975. He spent his first couple of years at Switzer's shuttling between the old factory, where it was still producing licorice the "old-fashioned" way, and the new plant with its experimental production line. His job was to document exactly how the licorice was made in the old plant so, if the new operation didn't work, they could go back to the traditional method.

Almost half a century after first joining Switzer's, Jim's enthusiasm has not diminished. He's a chemist, and his eyes sparkle when he talks about recipes, chemical reactions in food, and the entire process of solving complex problems of taste, appearance, and texture in the food industry. He speaks rapidly, so his words can keep pace with his thoughts.

His first step was to watch the men in the kitchen of the old factory mix the ingredients in the kettles. He knew there was a recipe and a process, and as a trained scientist he wanted to observe and record exact measures of ingredients, temperatures, and times. What he saw surprised him. "They'd put a little of this in it, and then a little of that, and in no particular order," he remembered. "And then they would just look at me and say, 'It's done!' I thought maybe they were having fun with me."

One man who worked in the kitchen with Jim described the process as "making it the way your gramma would." "And then I realized they were cooking the licorice until it achieved a certain shine on the surface," Clark said, noting that the perfect batch of licorice could not be created strictly by the book. That's because an essential element of the mix was flour and no two batches of flour could be the same because flour is made from wheat, and wheat is a plant, affected by rainfall, sunlight, and soil.

Mixing the licorice required the skills and instincts of an artist, which is what Joseph Murphy knew almost a century earlier when he mixed his butter, just a tad on the rancid side, into his caramels. The degree of subjectivity in the process was underscored by a story the kitchen workers would tell about how they would send tubs of cooled licorice to the upper floors for extrusion and occasionally have one rejected for poor quality. "So we'd take it back, let it sit for a day or two, and send it back up," recalled one old hand. "And the guy upstairs would usually phone back down to the kitchen, 'Yeah, that's more like it!'"

The second part of Clark's job was to assess the assembly line under development in the Broadway facility. With the new process, the licorice had to be made from a different recipe to compensate for the abbreviated workflow. The actual process was a simple one. The fluid mixture of candy ingredients passed through a cylinder, with a rotor churning the mix to make it touch the inside of the cylinder. Heated from the outside by steam, the cylinder wall cooked the candy and blades on the rotor cut the candy loose. That cycle continuously repeated itself, feeding the candy from the heat exchanger through a system of extruders, dies to shape the candy, and cutters to separate the pieces. A conveyor pulled the candy through a cooling tunnel to machinery that would package, box, and ship it.

It was hard to top the process for efficiency. The savings in labor was about 25 percent, but substituting a three-day process with a 20-minute one was bound to have a catch. Clark recalled, "When I first saw the product from the new process, it was pretty disappointing, because the packages had syrup in the bottom. They were just not salable. They were oozing syrup." There were other problems. The bites tended to stick together, and even though they came close to duplicating the black and red colors, the texture was off. The bites were shaped more like pillows than little cubes, and the Stix had lost their twist. The black licorice came out of the process looking more silky than shiny. Years later, Fred Switzer III, the founder's grandson, told the *Post-Dispatch*, "The taste and smell changed after my uncles and father sold Switzer's to Beatrice Foods."

Clark's job was to make it work. "I wanted to see what I could do to make this new process turn out candy that tasted like the old. And I did dozens and dozens of tests, changing the amount of flour and water and ingredients." No matter what he and his crew tried or how close they came, they knew it wasn't close enough to convince Switzer's licorice fans that they were eating the same candy they grew up with.

A 1980 Switzer's business plan referring back to those early stages admitted as much: "The product coming off the continuous process was not immediately accepted by the trade or the consumer." But Beatrice had invested a small fortune in the technology, and it needed to pay for its investment. The first product created from the continuous extrusion process and offered to the public were bites in February of 1976. The last of the open-kettle product were Stix, made in November of 1977.

"I hated to be a part of this," Jim Clark said many years later. "Beatrice had no feeling for the brand or the history. Just absolutely money. They just wanted to make money, and when they saw they had an inferior product out there, they didn't change."

As 1977 came to a close, the old factory, the home of Buttermels, Yellow Jackets, Chocolate Soldiers, Old Fashioned Licorice, and so many other candies since 1911, shut down. The lights went out, the doors were locked, and production shifted entirely to the new facility on Broadway.

Research and Development continued to experiment with different formulas and even brought in a licorice consultant from Europe. There were some improvements in the flavor, but the public was beginning to notice the difference and sales were starting to slip from what they had been in the days of kettles

Beatrice rolls out new products, 1977. Photo courtesy of Switzer's Licorice Archive.

and drying rooms. The marketing department pressed for new, innovative products. For a while Switzer's produced a licorice lace called the "Chew String" in the flavors Tangy-Orange, Strawberry, Cherry Red, and the traditional Black. They created the "Lariat", a 40-inch licorice rope suitable for both eating and twirling.

In 1976, Switzer's took the extraordinary step of importing a licorice candy from England. The new product came from a factory in the city of Pontefract, the original

Beatrice introduces "Albert Switzer," 1973. Photo courtesy of Switzer's Licorice Archive.

home of European licorice. The bite-sized licorice creams were packaged under the name of Switzer's Allsorts of Candy.

The trend of bringing in products from outside the traditional Switzer line continued in 1982 when Beatrice purchased the popular Good & Plenty brand and moved its production to the Switzer plant. Good & Plenty, created in the 1890s, is one of the oldest candy products in the United States. An earlier owner had replaced its chewy center with a soft, jellybean core, and sales were decreasing. Switzer's replaced it with the licorice center we know today and saved the little candy-coated pink and white licorice pellets from extinction.

While all of these internal changes were going on, the company's marketing folks experimented with a series of advertising efforts.

In the early 1970s, a cute little cartoon character, Albert Switzer Boy Explorer, assumed the role of company mascot. Albert's fame was short-lived though, probably because the public did not easily make the connection between the French theologian, philosopher, and medical missionary Albert Schweitzer—and licorice.

The company sponsored a chance to win an all-paid vacation for two to Switzerland. That too was short-lived, probably because the public did not easily make the connection between a small European country known for clocks, neutrality, and cheese—and licorice.

In 1979, Switzer's incorporated into its print advertising a cartoon strip called "The Adventures of King Chewy and Duncan the Switzer's Swiping Dragon." After a short time, the strip apparently ran out of plot lines.

Switzer's offered recipes to housewives looking for ways to spiff up meals with a touch of licorice. A favorite was Beef Barley Soup and Switzer's licorice bites.

Things were humming along with new products, sales were good, and Beatrice Foods was happy with its purchase of Switzer's. But Jim Clark and his team were still wrestling with problems related to the new continuous production process.

By the early 1980s, Beatrice had bigger problems than sticky licorice in St. Louis. The company had a long and distinguished history, going back to the 1890s when it developed a successful process of separating cream from whole milk. It grew slowly and cautiously into one of the nation's most traditional, non-controversial and successful traders of dairy and other food products. Headquartered in Chicago and governed by good, sensible Midwestern principles of responsible fiscal policies and a distinctly unflashy management style, the company became known for its practice of letting those closest to a problem solve it.

For years, William G. Karnes led Beatrice in a low-key manner that personified the company's reputation. But in 1979, leadership passed to James L. Dutt, whose autocratic personal manner and grandiose dreams of growth inserted greed into the company's mission. Decentralization and cautious acquisitions were a thing of the past. Beatrice ran up debts with risky purchases and the company became too big, sprawling, and unmoored. In 1980, a major reorganization consolidated 535 profit centers to 27. In 1982, Beatrice divested 50 of its companies to get back on its feet. Morale plunged, and from 1980 to 1985 Beatrice saw a mass exodus of the company's top executives, including Bob Kill, who was then a corporate vice president.

For most of its corporate life, Beatrice had received glowing and appreciative media coverage. Throughout the 1980s, it was a target of criticism for operating in South Africa during the time of apartheid. It was a co-defendant in a lawsuit alleging that a division of Beatrice dumped toxic waste into an aquifer that supplied drinking water to Woburn, Massachusetts. The case became the subject of a popular book and the film *A Civil Action*, starring Robert Duvall and John Travolta.

Sales in confectionery were still big, but not big enough for the new Beatrice. Less than two percent of Beatrice's $9 billion in annual sales were from candy, and catching up with Mars or Hershey was a pipe dream. There were rumors that Switzer's was tagged to be sold. A small group of Switzer's managers tried, without success, to buy the company. Bob Kill made his own offer, believing it was still a good brand and could succeed with better management than Beatrice was providing. But Beatrice had already made up its mind.

In December of 1983, Beatrice sold all seven of the candy companies in its Confectionery and Snacks Division to the

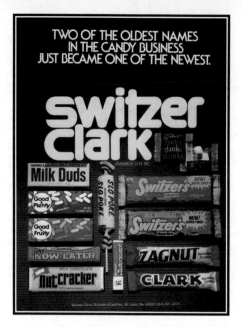

TWO OF THE OLDEST NAMES
IN THE CANDY BUSINESS
JUST BECAME ONE OF THE NEWEST.

Leaf promotes its new Switzer-Clark division, 1984. Photo courtesy of Switzer's Licorice Archive.

Finnish Conglomerate Huhtamaki Oyj, which combined all of its North American candy companies into a subsidiary by the name of Leaf. Leaf then created a division called Switzer-Clark, combining Switzer's line of products with those of the company that invented the Clark Bar. Consumers still saw the same products on the same shelves of their stores, but something new was happening in the candy business. Switzer's was now a small part of a conglomeration of companies owned by a company headquartered in Helsinki.

Switzer's new owner, Leaf, had once been a proud and independent American candy company before it was purchased by Huhtamaki Oyj. It first gained national popularity in the 1940s when it introduced Rain-Blo Bubble Gum, packaged with colored baseball cards. Then Leaf, like many small companies, went through a series of mergers and acquisitions to become one of the 10 largest candy producers in North America, playing the candy game on an international scale. Individual brands, each with its own history and nurtured by their creators, like Payday, Milk Duds, and Heath Bars, had become tiny elements in an international pool of brands with little value beyond the role they could play in grander marketing schemes. Now Switzer's Licorice was the new kid on the block. If there was any art left to the craft, it was in the branding, not the production.

But the deal was done. The new boss at Switzer's was a 32-year-old Helsinki native, eager to settle in St. Louis and apply the marketing strategies he had learned as a graduate student at Abo Akademi University in Finland. The *Post-Dispatch* reported that his objective was "to grow and grow rapidly and be able to compete against any of the big candy giants in all categories." If he made any specific comments regarding the quality of its products, they didn't make the news.

Over the next several years, Switzer's, in addition to making red and black licorice and Good & Plenty, would also produce Chuckles, Good & Fruity, and Jolly Rancher Mega Fruit Gummys.

Jim Clark remained in his job in quality control after the sale to Leaf. "This was an opportunity for us," he said. "Beatrice would not admit their mistake, that they damaged the brand, so we saw a chance to try to talk the new owners into at least going back partially to kettles."

Clark had been tinkering for more than 15 years with the continuous extrusion process for making licorice, and he was still not satisfied with the results. In April of 1991, he composed a lengthy memo to Leaf's senior vice president of marketing. He began the report by describing a visit he had made a few years earlier to the factory of a competitor by the name of Y & S, which made a popular licorice product called Twizzlers. The plant manager explained that Y & S's market share kept growing, "Because we make our licorice by an older and more labor-intensive method (open-kettle cooking), while our competition (Switzer's) uses newer methods that result in an inferior product." When Hershey's bought Y & S in 1977, Twizzlers came with the deal. Hershey's continued to produce it through the kettle method and consistently took a lion's share of the market.

Accompanying the memo, Clark attached a bar graph, showing that production of Switzer's licorice had declined from 23 million pounds in 1976 to seven million in 1985. "Switzer's volume was not taken away, it was given away," Clark argued in his report. "The damage was self-inflicted. Switzer's produces a product that the consumer perceives as inferior, and Switzer's has suffered and is suffering from the consequences."

The point of his memo was not to rail against past injustices to the product, but to present a nine-year plan to regain lost volume. He proposed bringing back the open-kettle system and combining it with more automated processes. He conceded that the continuous process might still be viable for certain products that would not be adversely affected by it. Y & S and Hershey's, he pointed out, had worked the same plan, paying for updates in its production facilities with money earned from taking away Switzer's volume.

But it's hard to see St. Louis all the way from Helsinki. Fortunately, Clark found an ally when Joe Scalzitti came down from Leaf's Chicago offices to manage the Switzer's plant in 1990. "Jim Clark was right," he recalled years later. "It was close, but you could still tell the difference between the continuous extrusion and the old kettle process."

With Joe's support, Jim doubled down on finding a solution. The company brought in new extruding equipment from Italy and applied new technologies that more accurately balanced the variables of heat and pressure. Because of the huge differences in St. Louis's seasons, Jim developed winter and summer recipes for the licorice.

But a critical element in reaching the solution was the input of the men and women operating the machinery. "It was teamwork," Joe recalled. "It was management, Jim's expertise, and the practical experience of the workers. Everybody worked together. And if the licorice didn't taste exactly the same as in the old days, you'd be hard pressed to tell the difference."

Production began to regain its old numbers, and within a couple of years Switzer's was producing from 12 to 14 million pounds of licorice a year.

That was the good news.

The bad news was that rumors began to circulate in 1996 that Huhtamaki was planning to sell the Switzer operation. In February, the company announced that it was moving its Good & Plenty production, one-third of the Switzer business, to Tennessee, a right-to-work state. Without Good & Plenty, the most profitable part of the operation, it seemed doubtful that the plant would remain open, and almost 300 employees would lose their jobs.

Teamsters Local 688 raised $13,000 to help finance a study of ways to keep the plant open. Teamsters International contributed an equal amount. A panel of professors from Northwestern, Columbia, USC, and MIT volunteered to study the situation and offered proposals, including the recommendation that Huhtamaki's subsidiary Leaf spend more money promoting the products. In September, the Finnish conglomerate rejected the union's proposals.

A headline in the October 18, 1996, Business Section of the *Post-Dispatch* read, "Switzer Candy Sold to Hershey." The Hershey Company paid $440 million to Leaf for a package of candy companies, including Switzer's. Leaf, in turn, bought Hershey's European candy-making operations for $110 million. Initially, no one knew what the purchase would mean for the workers.

Joe Scalzitti had led a small group of Switzer's managers attempting to buy the company before the sale. He kept his job as plant manager under Hershey's and continued to make offers to the company that was now employing him. He believed it was still a great product that deserved to be saved. It seemed like a good idea for everyone. Hershey's could unload a brand that competed with its own Twizzlers licorice brand, Scalzitti and his partners would save a historic St. Louis brand, the employees would keep their jobs, and the union would continue to take in dues.

Fred Switzer III made his own offer to Hershey's. He had opposed his family's sale to Beatrice years earlier and believed there was still life in the brand if it was properly marketed. Hershey's countered with a price so high he was convinced they had no serious intention of selling it.

After buying Leaf, Hershey's controlled one-third of the U.S. candy market. Twizzlers made up 60 percent of that market, while Switzer's weighed in at six percent. Hershey's saw no point in owning two competing brands and announced the following autumn that it would shut down the Switzer's St. Louis plant. Two hundred union employees offered to renegotiate their contract of $10 an hour with benefits, but Hershey's refused to talk.

On Friday, May 15, 1998, the last employee left the building at 1600 Broadway. The story of Switzer's Licorice had come to an apparent end. The event was marked by no fanfare other than a wistful article in the *Post-Dispatch*. No more factory. No more licorice. Nothing more than memories of a certain aroma that once hung over the landing. It was over.

View of abandoned factory from Washington Avenue. Photo courtesy of Kevin Manning for the St. Louis Post-Dispatch/Polaris.

CHAPTER NINE

Act of God

Switzer's Licorice left one conspicuous remnant of its life on the riverfront—a deserted red brick factory emblazoned with a fading painted sign facing the Gateway Arch. It seemed to be a likely candidate for rehabilitation. It was still a solid, dependable structure. Its rows of tall, arched windows and its Victorian design would fit well with plans to convert it into a stylish hotel or office complex. Its location on the southern edge of what remained of the historic manufacturing district offered a beautiful view of the Jefferson National Expansion Memorial to the south, an open eastern view of the Mississippi River, and a romantic nineteenth-century neighborhood with cast iron facades and cobblestone streets to its north and west.

There were lively discussions about the district's future even when the factory was producing licorice. As early as 1965, Fred Switzer Jr. led a group of property owners and businessmen calling themselves the Laclede's Landing Redevelopment Corporation to oppose a plan to raze the entire area and erect a group of high rises. The so-called River Center Plan and its artistic renderings of shimmering 50-story steel and glass towers got as far as being approved by the City Planning Commission in 1968 until cooler heads prevailed in city government.

The Laclede's Landing Redevelopment Corporation offered a proposal in 1975 that was unique among big-city urban renewal plans. Instead of buying property and waiting for the right tenants to come along, the strategy was to work with civic leaders and business owners, offering incentives, resources, and guidance over the next decade. The vision was to create a district of upscale retail, restaurant, office space, and entertainment venues within the nine square blocks between the river and Third Street, and the Eads Bridge and Martin Luther King Bridge to the north. The plan was approved by the City Development Agency, the Board of Aldermen, and the Mayor.

The district was placed on the National Register of Historic Places the following year, lending it a certain credibility. It was an important piece of the city—the last surviving patch of downtown that retained the original street grid of the village of St. Louis. It was the only portion of riverfront that had preserved the land's natural slope to the river. Many of its warehouses and factories were architectural gems, the last of their kind from the glory days of Victorian industrial design. And it was the only remaining neighborhood that offered a sense of how the entire industrial riverfront once appeared.

Shortly after Switzer's closed the factory in 1977, Edward and Donald Schnuck of the grocery chain family purchased it. They were impressed by its history and design but did not get as far as developing a clear plan or purpose for the old place. Several years later, a Houston developer drew up plans to convert it into offices and retail shops, but that fell through when the granting of federal tax credits became problematic.

In the early 1990s, several companies submitted proposals to develop riverboat casinos and create an entertainment district. One of the most promising was offered by Jumer Hotel and Casinos, which bought what developers had come to call "the Switzer Building" in November of 1992. Jumer's plan was to create an $80 million gambling complex on

Signs of neglect. Switzer building, 2006. Photo courtesy of Switzer's Licorice Archive.

the riverfront that would include two riverboats and the conversion of the factory into a 300-room hotel at a cost of $22 million. The deal offered the city of St. Louis seven percent of its gaming receipts. The city and the hotel were poised to sign the agreement in March of 1993 until a newly elected city administration added some extra conditions, which put the entire deal on hold and eventually killed it. It was the best plan the city would see.

As the years passed, the factory began to show more obvious signs of neglect. Even so, there was a steady buzz of plans and possibilities. The preservationist organization Landmarks Association optimistically removed Switzer's from its annual endangered buildings list in May of 1999, thinking it highly probable that it was only a matter of time until someone took on its renovation.

On a personal note, around that time I got an unexpected opportunity to get inside the plant for a self-guided tour. It came from an offhand remark I made to a friend who was associated with the Landing's Redevelopment Corporation. I mentioned that I had spent a lot of time in the factory as a kid, and he offered me the key to the front door and the advice to be careful not to fall through the rotten floors.

It was late afternoon, and the only illumination came from rays of light streaking in from the edges of the boarded rows of windows. It had the look and feel of a deserted church. The spaces that were once so busy and noisy were empty, shadowy, and silent. There was no smell of candy—just dust. I felt my way up a dark stairwell to the second floor and saw the spot that once hosted the office where my father and his father had worked. It was originally constructed as more of an afterthought than an actual office. It was just a couple of rooms attached, like a big box, to the wall, about 10 feet above the factory floor and accessible by a metal stairway. The only remaining trace was the old paint from the office walls, outlined against the red brick. It was too dark and dangerous to explore further. I looked for a small souvenir, like an exit sign or a doorknob, but there was nothing. The vandals and the ghosts had long given up this place, and whatever glory it once enjoyed had departed with them.

Local developer Pete Rothschild and a few partners created a company called Clarinet, LLC, in 2005 for the sole purpose of renovating the Switzer building. They called it Clarinet as a nod to the old musical slang term "licorice stick," which was used to describe a clarinet. Clarinet bought the factory from Jumer for $485,000, planning a $15 million renovation of the building into a mixed-use development called Switzer Lofts. The plan called for 28 condominiums, each in the $300,000 price range, street-level retail, a candy shop, a restaurant, and indoor parking. The state approved up to $50 million in tax credits in March of 2006, and it looked like the plan would move forward.

The old factory was in miserable condition, with a partially destroyed roof. When constructed in 1874, the building was

Fate on hold, 2006. Photo courtesy of Switzer's Licorice Archive.

designed so the brick exterior walls would support its weight. The walls were far too compromised by 2005, so Clarinet planned to construct a metal frame within the building that would offer the real support. By attaching the original bricks to the frame, the look of the original design could be preserved.

It might have worked if a freakish storm hadn't occurred the night of July 21, 2006. Winds reported at 90 mph tore bricks from the south wall and blew them across the Eads Bridge as the east wall collapsed. A report on the damage estimated that the storm damaged 80 percent of the interior structure and 65 percent of the exterior. The owners hastily erected scaffolding and anchored struts to the bridge to keep the rest of the building from collapsing.

Then the lawsuits began. Clarinet and its insurance company battled over who would pay for the damage. There was speculation of a plan underway to tear it down to the first two floors and build on top of it, but it became clear over the following months that the building was too far gone. Demolition began on the 133-year-old structure in May of 2007. Crews labored nights to avoid interrupting auto and train traffic on the bridge and it came down with no ceremony, few complaints, and surprisingly little media coverage. Small groups of preservationists, curiosity seekers, and mourners gathered to watch the process. It was as if its slow deterioration had been so pathetic and undignified that its final passing was almost a relief.

The city's preservation commission had expressed hope that its cast-iron facade could be saved, but the *Post-Dispatch* reported on May 25, 2007, that most of the six fluted columns were destroyed when the interior floors heaved forward and crushed them. The newspaper reported that workers chased off a would-be band of architectural thieves who pulled up in two trucks and tried to haul away one of the columns.

1874 cast iron columns along First Street entrance prior to demolition, 2006. Photo courtesy of Switzer's Licorice Archive.

"It was heartbreaking," Rothschild remembered. "We had an opportunity to do something that would leave a lasting legacy on the riverfront, but everything seemed to work against it."

When the ground was finally cleared, it was striking how small the lot really was, with just a patch of grass sloping toward Wharf Street and a few bricks scattered here and there. The Great Rivers Greenway District eventually purchased the land with plans to turn it into a recreational space for cyclists and hikers.

A beloved landmark was gone. Nevertheless, even until its last wounded days, it stood as a reminder of a time when the blocks along the river, with their factories, warehouses, and smokestacks, defined St. Louis as a noisy, gritty, bustling center of manufacturing.

Destruction of the old factory through an act of God would have made a wonderful finale to this tale. But there was more to come.

Damaged factory after the storm of July, 2006. Photo courtesy of Kevin Manning for the St. Louis Post-Dispatch/Polaris.

Nighttime demolition. Collapsed east wall, 2007.
Photo courtesy of Switzer's Licorice Archive.

CHAPTER TEN
Encore

There was no reason to believe that Switzer's licorice would ever again rejoin the world of candy brands. The licorice industry was dominated by two giant companies in the early 2000s. Hershey's had already bought and buried Switzer's, and the American Licorice Company was a powerful competitor with its Red Vine licorice. Between the two of them, they sold about $300 million worth of licorice a year, leaving little room for newcomers. Even getting products into grocery stores was a tough game, with major companies paying five figures just to have their products placed on shelves where customers could see them.

Michael Switzer was the grandson of candy company founder Frederick Switzer. His father was Joe, who developed an effective marketing network for the company with his golfing skills. Michael's background was advertising. In the 1980s, he co-founded a successful St. Louis agency, which he eventually sold, freeing him to pursue other creative enterprises. In 2001, he was researching the concept of "authentic brands" for a client selling a high-end auto wax. An authentic brand is one that traces its lineage directly to the original product and it occurred to him that he had a very close relationship to just such a brand.

"Being in the ad business for so many years, I really understood the power of a brand," Switzer recalled. "People have emotional connections with these authentic brands. And then it suddenly hit me that there was one out there right under my nose with some myth and some history to it, and I might be able to utilize that, so I started digging around to find out who owned the Switzer brand and develop strategies on how to get it back. Switzer's is a great American story."

He and his twin brother Joe hired an intellectual property attorney in 2003 to see if there were any obstacles to reclaiming the brand and bringing the Switzer products back to life. Under federal law, the Lanham Act of 1946 mandates that if a company does not use a trademark in the course of normal business for three consecutive years, it creates a legal presumption that the mark has been abandoned. Since Hershey's hadn't produced Switzer's licorice for about five years, the path seemed wide open for Michael and Joe. They spent the following year researching the market and scoping out the competition. Michael sought the advice of former Beatrice executive Bob Kill, who encouraged him. They managed to find the only existing copy of the original Switzer Licorice recipe and launched a national search for a company that could manufacture the products in a way that replicated the original taste. They chose a small family business in Minnesota that could manufacture up to 25 million pounds a year.

They showed up at the All Candy Expo trade show in Chicago in the summer of 2004, hawking their wares from a 10-square-foot canopy tent, surrounded by massive, sophisticated state-of-the-art displays by Hershey's, Mars, American Licorice, and the other giants of the candy industry. A few Hershey's representatives dropped by their booth and wished them good luck, but it was an almost comical version of David and Goliath. However, before the Expo had closed, the national chain of Cracker Barrel placed an order for 10 truckloads of their licorice. The Switzer boys had put their stake in the ground, declaring for all to hear that "Switzer's is back."

Meanwhile, Dan Warner, an entrepreneur and rehabber of historic buildings based in Webster Groves, was looking for a new project. He was considering buying a small candy operation in Ozark, Missouri, and asked Michael if he'd meet him for lunch at a local pizza parlor to give him some advice. They knew each other casually, having both attended Saint Louis Priory School as boys. Because the school had been co-founded by Michael's uncle, Fred Jr., Switzer's had regularly donated licorice to the school's snack

Switzer's Licorice partners Mike Switzer (left) and Dan Warner. Photo courtesy of Switzer's Licorice Archive.

shop. Dan and Michael shared the memory of snaking Switzer whips up their sleeves so they could munch on them in class, undetected by the monks.

Their business lunch turned into a four-hour event, until Michael finally asked, "Why would you want to buy that company when you could become a part of the Switzer's Candy Company?" Within months, Dan bought out Joe. Michael and Dan became partners in 2005.

During the first three months of their partnership, Switzer's sold more than $2 million worth of licorice. By the end of the year, the partners had, in addition to Cracker Barrel, added the grocery chains of Giant Eagle, Wakefern, Schnucks, Dierbergs, Straub's, and Shop 'n Save. Two other big accounts were Target and Kmart. Later they added Dollar Tree and its 9,000 stores.

They started with two traditional flavors, cherry and black, then added green apple, watermelon, lemonade, blue raspberry, and a strawberry flavor to compete with Twizzlers. They also added new candies, such as cinnamon and salted caramel flavored twists, and brought back the classic Buttermel.

The new Switzer's corporate office opened on the second floor of a building Dan owned in historic Old Webster. Michael's job was to keep his eye on the big picture, handling sales and customer relations. Dan, who was also a certified public accountant, took responsibility for operation and finances.

"When I think of Dan Warner as a partner, I always think of that scene in Butch Cassidy, when they come out at the end, flashing their pistols. And they never had to look over their shoulder to see if the other guy was shooting," said Switzer.

They've been a good team. Switzer knew how to position the brand and Warner, who had owned a small record shop for over 20 years, had practical experience slugging it out with giant competitors. "I came out of an environment in the record business where I was facing very large companies like Walmart and Best Buy, but I knew if we positioned our product differently, a certain amount of those consumers would appreciate that," he said.

And even though Hershey's and American Licorice had owned most of a $300 million dollar licorice market, Switzer's would only need a small piece of that to make it worthwhile. There were signs it could do it. A Baltimore newspaper columnist proclaimed Switzer's Licorice to be the "It" candy of 2005. Michael was invited to appear on a History Channel program that profiled business moguls from companies like

Switzer's Licorice supermarket display. Photo courtesy of Switzer's Licorice Archive.

New Switzer's product line. Photo courtesy of Switzer's Licorice Archive.

Tyson Chicken and General Electric. Mayor Francis Slay pledged Switzer's Licorice among a basket of St. Louis products in a World Series bet with Detroit's mayor.

There was one wrinkle. They believed they had done their due diligence in making sure the brand had been orphaned. They were convinced that they had the legal right to use it, even though they didn't have a document ensuring them of that right. Hershey's sent them a cease and desist letter in 2005.

While Michael and Dan felt they were prepared, this was a potential disaster. They were in full production, running an advertising campaign and selling licorice nationally. They hired an attorney and were prepared to defend their position, but the two parties decided to work out a business solution. Michael and Dan met with a group of Hershey's executives; by the end of the meeting everyone was satisfied, and Michael and Dan had secured worldwide ownership of the brand. "And that was a good thing because once we got control of the trademark, we felt we had our future in our hands," said Warner.

It's important to Michael Switzer that people know he is not driven by nostalgia. "A whole lot of people think I'm doing this for my grandfather or my father, but it's more about what these legacy brands mean," he said. "I'm not just doing it because it was Switzer's, but because those brands were going away and it's nice to see that we can keep them if we fight for them. It was a business decision and an appreciation for brands that have some real DNA."

That did not mean simply recreating what had already been done. Fred Switzer Sr. and Joe Murphy did not create a factory from a sense of nostalgia or romance. They made their decisions based on what they believed the public wanted. The goal was profit and the means was the creation of quality products. From the earliest days of cooking candy in a Kerry Patch Kitchen, through its eventual sale to Beatrice, Switzer's brands changed along with the public's tastes. More changes came when new technologies permitted the creation of new flavors, textures, and shapes. Penny candies and chewing gums gave way to chocolate and taffy products and eventually to licorice. Today a new generation of consumers demands less black licorice and more exotic flavors that zing and pop. "So, I don't see it as a retro brand. It's a relevant product with its own legacy that consumers want," said Switzer.

But candy has never been like any other manufactured product and never will be. As Warner explained, "Whenever you actually put a product in your body, your relationship with it is bound to be a special one. You need to trust it. You connect with it. And whenever you eat candy, you are enjoying yourself, so it connects you with good memories throughout your entire life."

Michael, the ad guy, agrees but sees it a little differently. For him, candy offers most of us the first choice we ever make as consumers. "Your parents give you a quarter and tell you that you can buy any candy you want. It's the first decision you ever make that involves a brand. So even as a kid, I had a sense of what the company was doing, because my dad was making the stuff that I was making choices about."

The company's distribution systems have been in a constant state of evolution from the first days of Fred Switzer peddling candy from a hand cart though the streets of Kerry Patch to deals with jobbers and their horse-drawn wagons, and, eventually, modern systems linking grocery and retail chains. Today a small company like Switzer's has the advantage of taking on the giants by creating branding campaigns conducted through the internet, and both Warner and Switzer cite that as part of the fun.

"Large brands like Hershey's and Mars once had total control of the distribution system," said Switzer. It was all top-down driven, and the consumer was a victim of whatever machinations these companies played, so when we walked into a store, we got whatever they offered us. It didn't matter what we really wanted."

The internet changed that, giving smaller companies like Switzer's the opportunity to make their own impact on the marketplace. Like the record industry, once controlled by giant companies that picked the stars it would create and promote, the candy industry could now bypass the old marketing and distribution systems and meet the consumers directly. The age of the Super Consumer, said Switzer, means his job is to "enhance the caliber and the quality of the product so that it lives up to the legacy, and the emotion and the myth of the Switzer brand."

"I made a licorice I like," he said with a wink. "Dan and I eat as much as we can, and we sell the rest."

Michael Switzer said one of his biggest regrets is that his grandfather died before he was born. And yet, he noted, he feels his presence every day as he takes the company through the perils and pitfalls that any small company encounters. Many are the same situations the original founders of the company encountered as they nurtured it through a changing business world.

"It's a challenging industry. We're up against monoliths—companies with more money than God. But it's fun to come up against situations, distribution, production, whatever it might be, and know that my granddad went through the same thing. I learn things for the first time that he learned for the first time, so Dan and I look at each other and say, 'I wonder what Fred Sr. said when he ran into this?' I feel like if Dan and I could sit down with the old guy we could have one hell of a conversation."

It's often the smallest things in life that mean the most. An aroma that claims a place in our memory and never leaves. A taste with the power to transport us back to our childhood. There is a certain silliness to candy. It is the most unpretentious of products. It claims to offer us nothing more than a burst of sweetness and the ability to make us smile. It's more fun to share than to enjoy alone, and so it brings us together. And how remarkable it is that an enterprise dedicated to such a fragile little item could endure so many years through wars and depressions, changing tastes, and the moods and temperaments of those who created it. The notion that a dream can be built upon candy is as strangely powerful as the fact that when it seemed to have died, it came back to life, bringing a touch of sweetness to our lives.

Frederick Michael Switzer, ca. 1890. Photo courtesy of Switzer's Licorice Archive

Family gathering. Fred Murphy's wedding, Webster Groves, 1918. Standing rom left, Joe Jr., his wife Josephine (who would die within a year of influenza), Helen (whose maiden name was also Murphy), Fred (peeking out from behind his bride), Margaret Switzer Murphy, her sister Aunt Nellie and the Old Gent. Seated, friends of the bride. Courtesy of the Murphy family.

AFTERWORD

Stories have the power to take us outside of time and let us wander through the past. I grew up in a house so thick with stories, I felt as if I knew people who had died before I was born. The tales had undoubtably improved with age, but in their own way they all took a stab at answering questions about where we came from and who we were.

We passed the best of them on from generation to generation, telling and retelling them the way we would play a favorite record over and over. Eventually the stories, like pieces in a puzzle, fit together to create a picture. It was a picture of us. Murphys and Switzers, famine and rebellion, passage to America, an Irish slum in America, and a candy factory.

Some years ago, I found among a box of items belonging to my parents a small, metal canister containing a reel of 8-millimeter film. It was labeled "December 1930." I had no idea what could be on it, but I couldn't get my hands on an old projector fast enough to find out.

If you are old enough to remember home movie nights, you also remember the projector's mechanical purr as it pulled the film from reel to reel. The film emitted a certain chemical aroma as it traveled past the hot projector bulb. In their day, these machines, beaming their flickering cones of light, transformed living rooms into other-worldly places.

All that came back in the instant I flipped the projector's switch.

It was a black and white home movie, shot in the front yard of my grandparents' house on Lockwood Avenue in Webster Groves. And because it was Christmas, most of the family was there. I recognized them easily from photographs I'd seen in family albums, but I had never seen them move, change their facial expressions, or relate to each other. It was as if they had come back to life.

The neighborhood had barely changed since 1930, so it was even stranger to see them in this very familiar place with wooden trollies and Model A Fords passing behind them on the street.

It was my family, but they were inhabiting a world of gray shades and silence as if they were ghosts but did not know they were ghosts. They seemed to be looking directly at me, even though they did not know me.

For over seven minutes they self-consciously perform little scenes for the camera. My grandfather Francis steals a kiss from my grandmother, and they both smile sheepishly. It's cold, and everyone is bundled up in coats and hats. Francis pulls his car into the driveway, gets out and points at it. His mother, Margaret Switzer Murphy, shuffles toward the camera and swoops up my startled, five-year-old father.

And then the entire screen is filled with the face of Joseph Bernard Murphy from Dublin, Ireland. He stares directly into the camera and then laughs. Maybe somebody said something funny. Maybe he just had to laugh at the silliness of making a movie. The camera goes to a wide shot, and now he is joined by his wife and his sons Francis, Joe Jr., and Fred.

They might have known that this could be their last chance to have a record of them all together with The Old Gent. They probably didn't care if anyone except them would ever see it.

Today I live one-half mile from their house and I pass it every day. It's always easy for me to see them standing there in the yard, posing and waving, barely concealed by all the layers of time between us.

Murphy-Switzer family plot at Calvary Cemetery, St. Louis.
Photo courtesy of the Murphy Family.

CO.

HOME OF

Switzer's
Licorice and
Cherry Red candy

A landmark captured in art. Portion of a
watercolor by St. Louis artist Marilynne Bradley.
Courtesy of Marilynne Bradley.

INDEX